Welcome to Motivate Your Child Action Plan

One of the most powerful things you can do as a parent is embrace the idea of *strategy* as you work with your child. Kids are people. They have hearts, and God is changing those hearts. How that change takes place is determined by many internal and external factors.

As you read through this book, you'll discover new tools and ideas to incorporate into your strategy for your child. We'll help you develop a specific, measurable plan to help your child change and move forward in life. This isn't one of those books you read through once and you're done. This book outlines a process that you'll use over and over again with each of your children.

Do we guarantee change? No, that would be unrealistic because your child isn't a robot under your will. However, even if change doesn't take place, we show you how to position yourself in such a way that you'll be doing all you can to influence change in your child.

If you haven't done so already, be sure to download the audio sessions from this site: www.biblicalparenting.org/actionplanaudio.asp.

Parenting is a process. It takes work and a lot of God's grace.

We've watched thousands of families experience greater closeness, cooperation, and overcome significant problems in their homes. You never know what specific tool or idea God might use to bring about change in your child. So do the hard work, and always be watching because God often surprises us with his grace in ways we never saw coming.

Enjoy your family. Even though the emphasis of this book is on change using strategies, plans, and techniques, make sure you take time to keep it all in the context of the love that God wants you to enjoy in your home.

Blessings,

Dr. Scott Turansky and Joanne Miller, RN, BSN

motivate your child
ACTION PLAN

Crafting the Unique
Strategy to Propel
Your Child Forward

Dr. Scott Turansky and
Joanne Miller, RN, BSN

PUBLISHED BY THE

NATIONAL CENTER FOR BIBLICAL PARENTING

First eBook release, January 2015
First Printing, January 2015

Library of Congress Cataloging-in-Publication Data

Motivate Your Child, Crafting the Unique Strategy to Propel Your Child Forward
by Dr. Scott Turansky and Joanne Miller RN, BSN
978-1-888685-68-8 (eBook) 1. Child rearing–Religious aspects–Christianity.
978-1-888685-67-1 (Paperback book) 1. Child rearing–Religious aspects–Christianity.

Turansky, Scott, 1957-
Miller, Joanne, 1960-

Title. BV4529.T88 1996 649'.1–dc22

The names of people who have come to the National Center for Biblical Parenting for counseling have been changed. Some illustrations combine individual stories in order to protect confidentiality. Stories of the authors' children have been used by permission.

A special thanks to Ron Wheeler of Cartoonworks for his illustrations.

The National Center for Biblical Parenting is a nonprofit corporation committed to the communication of sound, biblical parenting principles through teaching, counseling, and publishing written, audio, and video materials.

To obtain a complete resource list or have Dr. Scott Turansky and Joanne Miller present their material live, you may contact the National Center for Biblical Parenting 76 Hopatcong Drive, Lawrenceville, NJ 08648-4136, (609) 771-8002, or visit the website at: biblicalparenting.org.

You may also want to take online parenting courses at Biblical Parenting University. Learn more at biblicalparentinguniversity.com.

You may email us at parent@biblicalparenting.org.

Table of Contents

About the Authors

Dr. Scott Turansky and Joanne Miller, RN, BSN are the founders of the National Center for Biblical Parenting. Their heart-based approach to parenting is revolutionizing families. Turansky and Miller are also the creators of Biblical Parenting University, providing parents with easy access to parent training through online courses.

Scott Turansky is a full time pastor of Calvary Chapel Living Hope in New Jersey. He and his wife Carrie have five adult children and four grandchildren.

Joanne Miller is a pediatric nurse, working at the Bristol-Myers Squibb Children's Hospital in New Brunswick, New Jersey. She and her husband, Ed, have two grown sons. Joanne also works full-time leading the National Center for Biblical Parenting.

biblicalparenting.org
biblicalparentinguniversity.com
parent@biblicalparenting.org

1

Change in Forty Days

If there's something happening in your child's life that makes you feel uncomfortable, that's likely a good sign that change is needed.

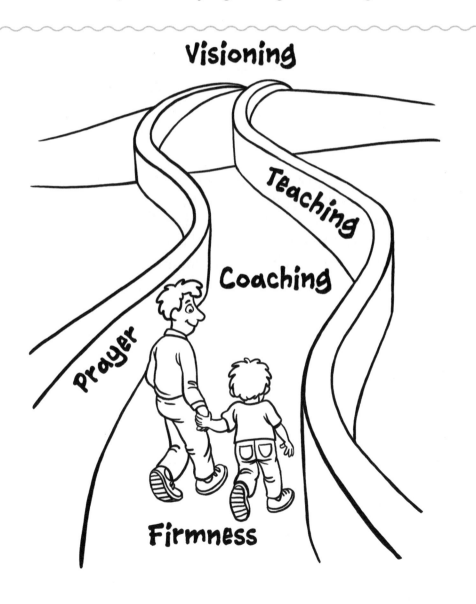

This is a strategy handbook for moving a child from where he is now to where he needs to be. In particular, we'll help you understand how people change from a biblical perspective. Then we'll show you how to develop godly strategies that will maximize the work you do with your child in order to bring about heart change.[1]

The heart is where God works. Change in the heart is much more powerful than behavior adjustment. Helping a child make heart-level changes requires an understanding of how God designed a person and how people function. It also means looking for new tools for your parenting toolbox that reach deeper than the surface. As you've probably realized already, relying on reward and punishment, as is commonly practiced, sometimes works for the short run, but often fails over time.

> Change in the heart is much more powerful than behavior adjustment.

Most parents know the importance of reaching a child's heart. In fact, as we start talking about the heart with parents, we see heads nodding in agreement. However, when we begin revealing the strategies that address the heart, the eyebrows come up as new ideas resonate. We all know how important the heart is, but we often don't know what to do with that knowledge when a child has a problem with lying or continually fighting with her sister.

We've dedicated our lives to the truth that a heart-based approach to parenting is the most effective, and we've developed hundreds of practical tools that actually address the heart of a child. If you ever get the chance to come to one of our live seminars or to a seminar presented by one of our many trained presenters, you'll hear ideas that will inspire and encourage you in your work as a parent.

Some people may be hesitant to read a parenting book or attend a parenting seminar because they think that they'll just go away feeling guilty, or that the ideas offered will be shallow or simplistic. It's because of this concern that we've placed great emphasis on plans and solutions. Parents leave our seminars hopeful

---

[1]You might like to read the Introduction of the book *Motivate Your Child: A Christian Parent's Guide to Raising Kids Who Do What They Need to Do Without Being Told* to learn more about how to bring about change using a heart-based approach.

and encouraged, armed with new techniques and strategies to help them work with their children. Parental encouragement is fueled by the reality that the ideas are consistent with a biblical understanding of how God created a person and how he works in our lives. The same is true for this book. The more you work through the chapters, the more hope you'll gain that there really are solutions.

Whatever the problem, the best solutions will embrace a heart-based approach. You can use this book to help you with almost any kind of struggle you're experiencing with your child. Here are just of few of the kids you'll meet in this book, each one needing some specific strategies and techniques to overcome challenges.

- Peter is eleven years old. He is angry and annoying to his sisters.

- Ten-year-old Lucy is disorganized and leaves messes around the house.

- Sara is eight. She is self-focused, demanding, and ungrateful.

- Becky is six years old and gets angry whenever she loses a game.

- Jason is fifteen years old. He is sarcastic and treats Dad like dirt.

- Michael has a problem with dishonesty and stole a toy.

- Emily is three and bites out of frustration.

- At seven, Corinne has Oppositional Defiant Disorder and is always resisting.

- Ralph is ten. He struggles with impulsivity and gets in trouble at school.

- Charlie is nine and lies about almost everything.

- Thirteen-year-old Brian faced paralyzing anxiety.

- At eight years old, Julianne is discouraged because God doesn't answer her prayers.

- Katie is fourteen years old and is bitter because she's often mistreated.

- Paul is nine and is mean to his mother.

- Jack is eight and continually gets in trouble for disrupting class.

- Max is eleven with Attention Deficit Hyperactivity Disorder and anger issues.

- Curt is twelve. He is irresponsible and unmotivated.

- Rick is twenty years old and is failing in life.

You'll also meet parents who came to some solutions for their children. Tim is learning how to mediate in the conflict between his wife and son. Richard is working on his harsh approach. Janene is learning how to give gifts of love to her daughter. Christina is tightening up on the sibling conflict between her three girls. Steve and Trudi are learning how to build internal motivation in their son. Brady wants to reach his wayward twenty-year-old.

This is a practical book, full of illustrations. The experiences are real, although we've combined some stories, changed the ages, names, or gender to protect the confidentiality of the families. Parenting is a challenge, and we enjoy walking the path with each family, helping them develop specific action plans to meet the challenges they face.

Many children have a combination of problems, further complicating the situation. That's understandable, and as you continue reading, you'll discover ways to identify the separate problems and bring solutions that will help in several areas at the same time.

Keep in mind that some of your parenting strategies will likely need to change. That doesn't mean that what you're currently doing is wrong. After all, there are a lot of good ways to raise children. But sometimes the good ways that parents use are not best for that particular child. We'll help you make adjustments, and you'll see improvement. In fact, with a good heart-based plan, you should see significant change in forty days. This isn't a gimmick. It's a reality. We work with many parents in counseling, both on the phone and in person, and it's amazing what happens in family life when parents embrace a heart-based approach.

> In fact, with a good heart-based plan, you should see significant change in forty days.

For those who might think that this is a book with a magic formula that changes any child in any situation, let's take a moment and look at some facts.

Fact #1: You are not ultimately in control of your child's heart. You've likely discovered that already. The Bible never says that a parent can change the heart of a child. Only two people can change a person's heart. One is God himself, and the other is the person who needs to change. The latter is called "repentance" or a change of heart or mind.

Fact #2: A parent can have a strong influence to guide and lead a child to a point of change. That's why a good parental plan is important. Brady is a good example. Rick, his son, is twenty years old now, can't hold a job, is attracted to marijuana and alcohol, and is generally failing in life. Does that mean that Brady has failed as a parent? Brady would admit that he made some mistakes, just like the rest of us, but wallowing in guilt for past mistakes won't motivate his son to start making right choices in his life.

Brady is committed to reaching the heart of his son, Rick, The tools offered in this book provide him with wisdom as he meets each new parenting challenge. Rick will have to make some right choices in order to move forward. Dad, however, is positioning himself well to parent his son, often adjusting his plan to meet new twists and turns in the path.

Fact #3: Children are people, not robots, and each child has a heart from which the decisions of life flow. As Brady continues to rely on the Lord, he will discover new tools and ideas. As he continues to rely on a fresh work of the Spirit in his own life, God will provide Brady with strength to work with his son.

It's with an attitude of humility that we move to the first step in the process.

The Important First Step

Before you move forward to develop an action plan for your child, take a moment and pray. As you pray for your son or daughter, God will do some things in your own heart as well as in your child's. Your anger will decrease, thoughtfulness will increase, and you'll likely see some change in your relationship with your child even before you start developing your plan. As you continue to embrace solutions, you'll find that prayer isn't only important as you start, but it's also necessary all the way through. You'll read about praying for your child, with your child, and how to teach your child to pray and ask God for the power to change as well. Prayer changes things. It's God's idea. We must start there, or we'll begin to think that we are totally responsible for the change. When that happens, pride or discouragement can ruin the plan.

Take a moment and reflect on the importance of prayer. Make a list of three things about your child that you'd like to present to God.

1. _____

2. _____

3. _____

Many parents come to a book like this one looking for more consequences to use with their kids. You will get some ideas in that department, but you'll also learn many more tools that will prompt change more deeply and completely. Some of the plans described in this book will increase pressure on your child. So, it's important to remember that kids can only take as much pressure as the relationship allows. As you pray, ask God to increase relational platforms on which he can build your strategies. We'll give you more specific ways to strengthen that relationship as part of your plan, but for now, just pray that God will do a work in you, in your child, and in the other members of your family.

When you look at the list that you just made about your child, how many of the three things were negative, things you'd like to change? Although it's very appropriate to ask God for change in your kids, it's also important to thank the Lord for specific things that make your child unique and special. For example,

a child who tends to be flexible may also be messy, or a child who is great with art might not do so well at math or science. The same is true with character and personality. So, before you go on, list three things that you value about your child and write those three things here.

14

1. _____

2. _____

3. _____

As you consider change, sometimes the end results appear to be so far off that discouragement sets in. In this book, we're looking for change in a relatively short period of time. A good plan can often see some change in the first few days and significant change in forty days. But it takes strategy, quite a bit of work, and a heavy dose of God's grace, all at the same time. Why did we choose forty days? Because that's a common time frame in the Bible that took place at significant transition points. Here are some examples:

1. It rained for forty days and forty nights when God wanted to cleanse the world and start over (Genesis 7:12). A significant transition in our world history.

2. Moses was on the mountain with God for forty days and forty nights to receive the Ten Commandments (Exodus 34:28). A transition to following the law.

3. It took the spies forty days to search out the Promised Land and bring back fruit (Numbers 13:21-25). A transition looking forward to the new life in Palestine.

4. God prompted Elijah to walk for forty days to the cave where he would learn that God speaks in a quiet whisper, not just in dramatic ways such as fire from heaven (1 Kings 19:3-18).

5. Jesus fasted for forty days and forty nights in the wilderness (Matthew 4:1-2). The transition of Jesus into earthly public ministry.

6. Jesus was seen on the earth forty days after his crucifixion (Acts 1:3). The transition to the Church living without Christ on this earth among them.

Will children be totally transformed in forty days? That's unlikely, but you can expect to see encouraging signs of improvement. An important transition will take place in your child, and even small steps of change will provide hope that will drive you forward.

In order to work on a particular area of your child's life, you'll need to focus on it, pray, meet with your child, and develop plans. You'll likely have some corrective moments, training exercises, and discussions. Change will require time. You'll have to organize your life in a way that will provide enough margin in your schedule to allow for the extra work required by you.

What changes do you think might need to take place in you and your family's schedule in order for you to concentrate on a particular issue in your child?

_____

_____

_____

_____

In one sense, forty days doesn't seem very long. That's less than a month and a half. But when you're in it day after day, trying to work your plan and making it a high priority, it's a long time. It's hard to change patterns of anger, bickering, complaining, or disrespect. But the small steps of change become huge strides as you focus on an area and watch for improvement.[2]

Likely, the change in your child will require change in you. When parents

---

[2]You might want to read Chapter 19 in the book *Motivate Your Child: A Christian Parent's Guide to Raising Kids Who Do What They Need to Do Without Being Told* to learn more about how your home is a discipleship center. This chapter also shares four areas of theology that are important for children to learn.

change the way they parent, kids have to change the way they live. There are lots of good ways to raise a child. Maybe the good things you're doing aren't working because they aren't the best for this particular child. Often, a new approach or a novel method can remove roadblocks.

> Likely the change in your child will require change in you.

In fact, we often find that God provides parents with keys to change. It's hard to know exactly what they are when you start, but as you rely on the Lord and study your child, fresh strategies are revealed. The goal of this book is to help you think outside the box and develop new ideas and approaches that you hadn't thought of before. You may try different techniques before you land on the best ones that will bring about change.

Occasionally it's something simple that makes the greatest impact; one conversation, one approach, or one technique. Many times, however, kids need a multifaceted plan for change. This book will outline the various things to consider when building an effective plan.

Take Martha, for example. Her eleven-year-old son, Peter, was particularly challenging, often defiant, angry, and obnoxious with his sisters. Martha continually confronted him, tried to remain calm but firm, and took his iPad away as a consequence. She saw little improvement. There's nothing particularly wrong with her approach. It had worked with her daughter in the past. We might even have recommended that kind of approach ourselves, but it wasn't working.

Martha was ready for a change. We guided her to some new ideas, and here's what she ended up doing. She met with Peter and asked for help. "I want to have a close relationship with you. I'm feeling like the way we're navigating through life isn't working. Let's look at our mornings. I wonder if together we could come up with a plan that would reduce the tension we both feel. I value you, and I think we can develop more of a team approach as we're trying to get through our morning routine. I'm hoping you might brainstorm with me some ways that we might do that."

Peter had some ideas. "You could stop nagging me in the morning. You pick on me and not my sister when something bad happens, and you add more things to my to do list in the morning when I'm trying to get myself ready."

Mom took a deep breath. "Okay. Those are a lot of things you'd like me to not do. What can I do? I'm still the mom, and I have to make sure you get out the door having accomplished what needs to be done."

It was at that point that the conversation changed. Peter actually had some helpful suggestions. They created a list of the tasks Peter needed to get done before going out the door. It was decided that Peter would manage the list. Mom would check the list a few minutes before they had to leave. They determined to do better the next morning, and they did. To Mom's surprise, Peter, on his own initiative, chose to take the laundry down instead of playing on his video game. That shocked her because she didn't imagine that her son was capable of such thoughtfulness. They were off to a great start. The next few weeks had some challenges. Some days didn't go very well, but Mom and Peter talked about the problems and made adjustments.

> It's not about taking solutions from another family or finding an easy fix. This book is about developing a strategy for change.

The plan worked because Martha changed her approach. She expressed value for the relationship, invited critique, and made it clear that she was still in charge. She determined an arena where they would work on the problem and asked for cooperation with a sense of teamwork.

That approach doesn't work for all kids, but it worked for Peter. Mom found the keys that her son needed to bring about change. It was a Peter-solution, and it required they both make adjustments in order to move forward.

In this book, you'll learn how to develop a unique plan for your child. It's not about taking solutions from another family or finding an easy fix. This book is about developing a strategy for change.

Crafting a New Approach

When parents try to change patterns of behavior with their kids, they often need several ideas, not just one. It's more than simply finding a new consequence or having one significant talk with your child. Rather, you'll want to build a structure for change. By positioning yourself well when the challenges present themselves, you are more likely to motivate change in your child.

This is a book of tools, but more importantly, it gives you a framework for creating your own plans. You may do some research, get ideas from friends, and even ask your kids for solutions, but they'll fit within the outlines we've developed here.

As you work through this book, you'll see several elements that make up a good plan: relationship, firmness, visioning, spiritual strength, teaching, and coaching. Each of those elements is developed in its own chapter. In addition, you'll see references to the book, *Motivate Your Child: A Christian Parent's Guide to Raising Kids Who Do What They Need to Do Without Being Told*, offering helpful insights and tools you'll likely want to consider.

Living daily with the challenges of conflict and chaos can be overwhelming. In some cases, just pulling back and looking at the situation can provide some perspective. That's what Moses wanted to communicate to the Israelites when they were under pressure from the pursuing Egyptians. They had left Egypt but didn't know exactly how to get where they were going. They just knew that they wanted to get out of there. It reminds me of how many parents feel regarding the problems their children have. As the Israelites approached the Red Sea, they had water in front of them and an advancing army behind them. They were under pressure, and they complained and worried for their lives.

In that moment, Moses spoke up. He brought hope into the situation in Exodus 14:13-14, "Moses answered the people, 'Do not be afraid. Stand firm and you will see the deliverance the Lord will bring you today. The Egyptians you see today you will never see again. The Lord will fight for you; you need only to be still.' "

The Israelites, in that moment, needed a new perspective on their challenging situation. Actually, they needed a God-perspective. And the Lord wants to do that with you, as well. It's going to be hard work, no doubt. But keep in mind that God is in control, that he provides wisdom, and that he gives grace. Step back a bit, do the work necessary to figure out your situation, and then allow God to provide a new approach. Remember that every child is unique, both with strengths and weaknesses. Interests differ and keys to motivation vary among children. In the next chapter, you'll study your child in order to determine some basics before moving forward.

Have a Meeting with Your Child

As you develop an action plan to help your child grow in a particular area, take time to share it with your child. Of course, how you communicate the plan is part of the strategy and can mean all the difference between success and failure of the plan. Each chapter of this book will give you ideas for a meeting you might have with your child. Sometimes you will announce the meeting in advance and schedule it with your child. Anticipating a scheduled meeting can be helpful and communicates its importance. Other times, you'll watch for that teachable moment and be ready to take advantage of it when it happens. In either case, this book will give you practical suggestions of things you might say and ways you might communicate with your child to bring about change.

In the first meeting, you might want to communicate the problem in general terms. At this point, don't define your child's problem, make threats, or somehow weaken the power of the subsequent meetings. Rather, simply communicate two things: sadness and a wish. Remember that this is only one of several meetings you'll have. Some parents make the mistake of trying to solve the whole problem in one meeting. The more complicated or ingrained a problem is, the more likely it is that you'll need several parent/child meetings to motivate your child to change.

> Rather, simply communicate two things: sadness and a wish.

Sadness and a Wish

First, you'll want to express sadness over the problem. Sadness that your relationship together is strained or sadness that your child is not being successful. It's not about being disappointed with your child. Rather, it's a sadness that your child likely also feels, but may not know how to communicate. This type of empathy raises the awareness level about the critical nature of the problem. Often, relationships are being damaged, or kids are miserable.

Then, express a wish that things could be different. No details. No specific plans. Just sadness and a wish. You might say, "Son, I'm sorry we're having such a significant problem whenever I ask you to do something. I can see that it's upsetting for you, and you sometimes respond with resistance. It's also upsetting for me, and I sometimes don't know what to do. I wish we could find some solutions that would make things easier for both of us."

Another option might be, "Jill, I notice that, when it's time to do chores, like clearing the table, you tend to find something else that you need to do at that moment, leaving me working on the chores alone. I wish we could develop a plan where you help me with some of the chores around our home."

Or it might look this way. "Honey, I can see you're struggling with the truth sometimes. I wish I could help you develop a solution that would enable you to overcome the habit of lying."

Obviously, this isn't the full extent of your plan, but you're raising the awareness level and you're communicating a caring attitude and a desire to help. Future meetings will be more specific, and your existing discipline will need to continue, but this first meeting lets your child see that change is in the air. You'll be back with more later, but the first meeting prepares the way and, in

many cases, starts building hope, a necessary ingredient for the heart to change.

Take a moment and journal here about the meeting. Don't write about what didn't work. Rather, jot down ideas that did, things you'd like to remember of future meetings, and what you learned.

How did your meeting go? What did you learn? What worked?

_____

_____

_____

_____

_____

_____

_____

_____

Where Do You Want to Go?

Change is the key to growth, and growth is the evidence of life.

I f it looks like disobedience, sounds like disrespect, and feels like abuse, then there's definitely a problem. But just telling kids to be quiet, stop arguing, and cut out the back-talk may not be the most effective approach. Kids need to know what to do instead and need tools to get there. So do parents. Let's take some time and create a map to understand where you are now and where you need to go.

> If it looks like disobedience, sounds like disrespect, and feels like abuse, then there's definitely a problem.

If you're looking for canned solutions that you can simply implement, you won't be as effective as if you plan a specific strategy for your child. Every child is unique and, if your plan is tailored to your child, you'll be far more successful.[3]

A good place to start is with what you already know. Most of the time, parents are quite familiar with the problem. They see it every day and experience the consequences continually. Let's start right there. Any good problem-solving strategy begins with defining the problem. In fact, you might want to journal for a few days, simply trying to figure out what's going on. Use some of the ideas that follow to study your family in general and one of your children in particular.

Step #1 – Identify the Problem

In the spaces below, take a few minutes and jot down specific behaviors that your child exhibits that demonstrate a problem. What things is your child doing wrong? If you need more writing room, then get out a piece of paper, or maybe it's time to get out a notebook where you'll take notes, jot down ideas, and formulate your specific plan. List behaviors, not analysis or root causes. For example, you don't want to write down, "He's selfish," but rather, "Won't share his toys." You might write, "Yells at his brother to get out of his room," instead

---

[3]You might read Chapter 1 in **Motivate Your Child: A Christian Parent's Guide to Raising Kids Who Do What They Need to Do Without Being Told** for additional understanding about how a parent can develop the conscience of a child and teach that child to use Level 2 thinking, which focuses on responsibility.

of "He's mean." Don't analyze yet. Just make observations.

This is not a list that you'll show your child. However, the items on the list are things that your child would recognize. These are the actions that get him into trouble, and he needs a plan to address them. Later, you'll take individual parts of this list and share them with your child in a hopeful way, but for now, just write down the evidence.

\
\
\
\
\
\

Step #2 - Categorize Common Challenges

Once you've added several items to your list, try to group these behaviors around common issues. You're looking for patterns, not one-time mistakes. Put a mark by several that are similar problems and a different mark next to a different group of behaviors. Try to name each concern. For example, you might see several actions that illustrate selfishness, and different actions that result from lack of organization. This task alone often provides hope for parents because now, instead of fifty problems to work on in the form of behavior, you've identified three or four areas of concern.

Don't be in a hurry to complete this part of the process. Some parents take a few days to study their child and evaluate the situations. Others find that the process moves pretty quickly and the solutions are easy to define. Some children are quite complicated, and so "figuring them out" takes time.

For example, one mom found that her son, who generated a lot of conflict in the mornings, had some other issues going on. Through the discovery process, she listened to him, and he said, "I don't know why I feel so frustrated when I get up. I'm irritated." That one comment revealed an underlying issue that led her to a different solution than she had originally planned.

As you ponder the groups of behaviors, what might you call each group? For example you might use the word "self-focused," "mean," "unorganized," or "angry." You won't want to use these as labels for your child, but you will want to keep them in your mind as you move toward your target. Jot down here one or two key words that sum up your child's weaknesses.

You're getting closer to the place where you can start working on a plan, but not yet. You need a bit more analysis before you can move forward. These first steps are helping to define the problem more clearly.

Step #3 – Specify the Target

Now that you have a list of the behaviors and you've grouped them into categories, ask yourself this question: "What character quality does my child need to develop in order to grow in this area of life?"

A character quality, for our purposes, can be defined this way:

A character quality is a pattern of thinking and acting in response to a challenge.

It's the challenge that reveals either the character or the lack of it. Your child experiences internal challenges and doesn't have a good plan for addressing them. One child may get angry with his brother when his brother is annoying. Another child may lie to get out of trouble. Another may blame problems on others and not take responsibility. In each case, these children are facing challenges without a good plan to address them.

As we look at the definition of a character quality we recognize that it has to do with tendencies. Character is a pattern of thinking and acting. The child who is patient thinks and acts differently than the person who is impatient. The person who has integrity reacts differently than the person without that character trait.

Your goal over the next few weeks is to equip your child to think and act differently when faced with particular challenges. The plan you create will help your child develop new tendencies or patterns of thinking and acting. So, consider the character quality the target of your plan that's necessary in order to overcome the challenges.

I'M LOST. I NEED SOME HELP.

Take Lucy, for example. She is ten years old and needs to develop thoughtfulness instead of being self-focused, kindness instead of meanness, and neatness instead of being disorganized. Her parents will take those issues one at at time, but for our purposes, let's look at the last one. Lucy's messiness comes from a lack of one or more of these qualities: hardworking, thoughtful, or neatness. By choosing one of those, her parents move into a specific set of patterns in their training. As you think about your child, you might want to avoid a quality like responsibility that basically covers everything you want your child to grow in, unless you're going to define it in specific terms.

Take a few moments and analyze the data from your list and write down three or four character qualities you'd like to see your child develop that correspond to specific weaknesses. (There's a list of character qualities at the end of this chapter if you need some ideas.) Keep in mind that, if you've been using a word over and over again with your child, such as kindness, then you will likely want to change it to a related word such as thoughtfulness, because of the negative association your child may have developed. That isn't always necessary, but a different approach can often be strategic.

Write down a few character qualities you'd like to see as targets for your child's heart. Obviously, you could describe the ideal child here and write down every good quality that comes to mind. Rather, think of the problems at hand, and identify just three or four qualities that might address those challenges.

_____

_____

_____

Step #4 – Define the Character Quality

> Look for ways to define the quality so that your child can understand it.

Now it's time to create a working definition to describe what this character quality means for your child, what it will actually look like. A working definition is a way of putting hands and feet to the term. Look for ways to define the quality so that your child can understand it. This is not a dictionary definition but a practical description of what that quality looks like in real life. The definition might be different for another child, but you're making the character quality relevant and practical for your child.

Here are some examples:

Sensitivity means that, when I walk into a room, I look and listen before I speak. Thinking about how my actions affect other people is important. Sensitivity means thinking about how I could help someone else.

Thoughtfulness (in response to the lack of organization in the above example) means that I pause before leaving a room to check to see if anything needs to be straightened up before I leave.

With these kinds of working definitions, you're helping to clarify how your child should think about the challenges and the solution. On the lines below, choose one of the qualities from your list and create some working definitions tailored specifically for your child.

Step #5 – Identify the Arena

You want progress to be measurable. For that reason, you'll want to choose an arena where you and your child will work on this quality. The arena is where the action takes place. A sports arena hosts completion between two opposing players or teams. In the same way, competition takes place in your child's heart between common challenges and a growing character quality. A battle takes place in the heart before you see the outcome in the behavior.

> You want progress to be measurable.

While looking at your previous behavior list in Step #1, identify one arena where your child can work on the new plan. For example, you might want to work on self-control in the arena of following instructions, or kindness in the arena of playing with his brother, or sensitivity when tempted to talk out in class. In our example of messiness, you might choose homework, the bedroom, or the kitchen as the arena.

By choosing the arena, you're creating a workspace where the new plan will be implemented and practiced. Take a moment and write down the character quality from the previous step #3 and the arena where you'll want to work on it.

Remember, you're working with a person, and that person has a heart. The heart is a complex place. Proverbs 20:5 says, "The purposes of a person's heart are deep waters, but one who has insight draws them out." You're trying to figure out the "insight" part of that verse. The challenges your child faces are in the heart before they come out in the behavior. What will it take for your child to win the battle in the heart first? As you continue to develop your plan, you'll make changes based on new insights you discover.

Have a Meeting with Your Child

How information is communicated to your child is critical. Now that you've done your homework, jot down some notes on a piece of paper, close this book, and plan your meeting. These notes will give your interaction the best chance of a positive response, but keep in mind that, even if you don't get a good response from your child, you can still work your plan. It's your goal in this meeting to do your best to get your child onboard with, and maybe even contribute to, the plan. Here are some hints for making this meeting most successful.

1. Don't have this meeting at a discipline time. Although the solutions will help address some of the discipline situations, you want this meeting to be positive. So, either take your child out somewhere, wait for a responsive moment, or set an appointment with your child to get together and talk.

2. Present the information in a positive and hopeful way. Essentially you're saying to your child, "I've been pondering the problem you're experiencing, and I have an idea that I think can help you." A hopeful approach often wins over a child who might otherwise be resistant or defensive. Your hopefulness is contagious. Your goal is to communicate a team approach to overcome the problem.

> By choosing the arena, you're creating a workspace where the new plan will be implemented and practiced.

3. Keep the meeting brief. Too much information can overwhelm a child and may be counterproductive. If the meeting leads to a significant conversation, go with it, but don't talk on and on. The purpose of this meeting is to introduce a solution. You'll go into more details in a subsequent meeting.

4. Start by sharing the positive character quality and why you believe it will be helpful for your child. Talk about the arena where the challenges are typically faced. Don't spend a lot of time rehashing the child's

misbehavior. You'll likely want to share some of the working definitions of the character quality you came up with. Maybe even ask for input from your child of what this would look like.[4]

5. You could end the meeting here, or together you could look for ways to post the quality around the house or gather more definitions, depending on the responsiveness of the child.

6. Over the next few hours and days, talk about the character quality, point out positive examples, and raise the awareness of its practical benefit. When misbehavior takes place, raise the awareness that this quality is the solution. Simply making an observation such as, "Here's a time when thoughtfulness would really help you." Or, "Here's that challenge you're facing in your heart. It would be a good time to consider thoughtfulness."

Although just one meeting may be all that some children need to start making changes, most children need further work. Some even need a rather elaborate plan to move forward. Be careful that you don't just have one meeting and think you're done. Talk about the character quality in life and discuss progress made. It takes some work to change tendencies of the heart, both for the child and for the parent. Over the coming days, continue to raise the awareness of the quality and its application, trying to balance pressure with encouragement in order to see progress. The next chapters will guide you to deeper heart-based solutions and add motivational components that are often needed.

Some parents see progress in their child as a result of this first meeting. As you see positive steps, be sure to point them out. A little affirmation can go a long way to guide a child's heart. Momentum builds as you move forward.

It's amazing to see some children change quickly with this kind of approach. Let's take a real example of a problem mentioned earlier in this chapter. Lucy, at age ten, was quite disorganized, often leaving messes around the house. When her Mom and Dad shared the solution of thoughtfulness with her, she grabbed onto the idea. Things started to change rather quickly for her. All she needed was

---

[4] You might want to read Chapter 2 of *Motivate Your Child: A Christian Parent's Guide to Raising Kids Who Do What They Need to Do Without Being Told* for more ideas of how to maximize the power of your words.

a new way of looking at life.

Not all children or their problems will change as quickly as Lucy. Some kids need a rather complex plan with multiple meetings in order to change. Please don't be discouraged if your child doesn't respond instantly to various parts of the plan. Just keep reading, working, and adding new components as you go. We'll help you develop a multifaceted plan for change with several forms of motivation to move forward. On the other hand, recognize that some kids just need a new way of looking at life and, once presented, it opens the heart to significant change. It has to do with those keys to the heart. You never know what the Spirit of God may do at any given time. Be ready and prayerful.

> If you see any signs of success, then celebrate them with praise and affirmation.

If you see any signs of success, then celebrate them with praise and affirmation. If you don't, then move to the next chapter for more ideas. One sixteen-year-old boy reported it this way, "I didn't see any change in my ability to handle my anger for a couple of months, then I had a breakthrough and things started changing quickly." So, hang in there. Don't get discouraged. There are many more pieces to the plan that are yet to come.

How did your meeting go? What did you learn? What worked?

_____

_____

_____

_____

_____

_____

_____

_____

_____

List of Character Qualities

adventurous
ambitious
calm
carefree
caring
cautious
cheerful
clever
contented
confident
cooperative
courageous
creative
curious
dependable
determined
forgiving
friendly
fun-loving
funny

generous
gentle
hard-working
helpful
honest
humble
imaginative
independent
inventive
joyful
kind
loving
loyal
mannerly
neat
obedient
organized
outspoken
patient
patriotic

playful
pleasant
polite
quiet
reasonable
resourceful
respectful
responsible
sensitive
sentimental
serious
sharp-witted
studious
thoughtful
tough
trusting
understanding
unselfish
wise

3

The Map to Get There

Parents are like tailors, specializing in alterations. The challenge is making the design fit for each unique person.

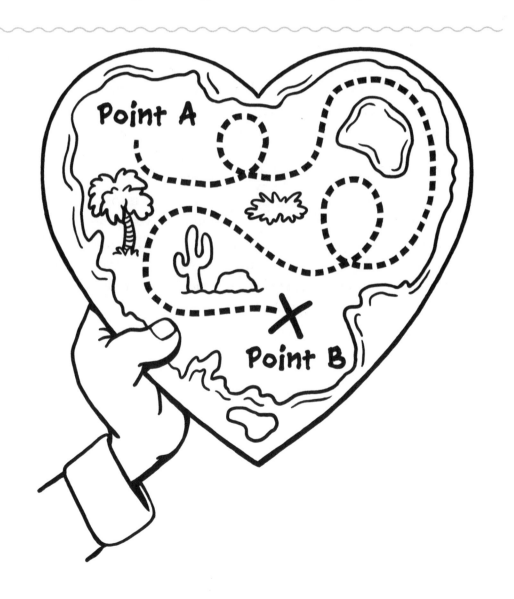

Recently, we were invited to speak to the New York Yankees Major League baseball players and their wives about parenting. We started our time by saying, "We're going to suggest to you some strategies and techniques for working with your kids." Ball players understand those two words: strategy and technique. It helped us connect with our audience in that case, but the same truth is important for anyone.

Effective parenting contains three different components: 1. Good theology, 2. Strategy, and 3. Technique. Good theology includes understanding how God made a person, how God designed relationships and the world itself, and the fact that God has a plan that involves each of us and our children. These are the same for all of us and understanding good theology is an important foundation for maximizing change in a child's life. Too many parents miss this and try to move on to the others without a solid biblical foundation.

The second component is strategy, specific ways of thinking how to move a person from where he is to where he needs to be. These strategies are unique for each person and require that you study your child, figure out where the roadblocks are that prevent growth, and then provide an overall plan to lead the child forward. The third component is technique. These are the tools that, when used wisely, can help make the strategies work.

Many parents want techniques without working through the other components first. That can be a mistake, and they flounder around from technique to technique, looking for one that might bring about change. There are a lot of good techniques out there, but the best one for your child will come from strategies, which come from insight and wisdom, and are often much broader in scope.

When Dora caught this concept, it changed the whole way she worked with her eight-year-old daughter, Sara. We first met Dora when she brought this concern to us. "My daughter is demanding and only thinks about herself. She's not grateful for anything and always wants more. It's as if the whole world revolves around her, and if she doesn't get what she wants, then she gets angry.

No matter what I take away or how I reward her for good behavior, we still see the same problems over and over again."

We helped Dora with Sara, but we didn't start by simply giving her another technique. First, she needed to understand some good theology about how people change, and then we helped her develop a strategy for her daughter. More on Dora's situation in a moment, but let's first look at some key ideas that all parents, including Dora, need to know.

A Map Mentality Changes a Parent's Perspective

Parents who don't embrace a good strategy often use what we call "Reactive Parenting." They see a problem and just react to it. No plan seems to be present except to communicate their displeasure, and their techniques are used haphazardly. It's our desire to bring some structure and direction to your approach so that you can maximize the influence you have in your child's life.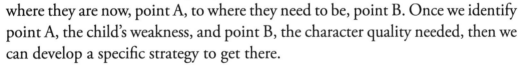

In order to help children change, it's important to view their hearts on a map that takes them from where they are now, point A, to where they need to be, point B. Once we identify point A, the child's weakness, and point B, the character quality needed, then we can develop a specific strategy to get there.

Unfortunately, many parents don't use a map mentality. Instead, they use a justice approach often characterized by an if/then chart. They basically say, "If you do this, then you get this, and if you do that, you get that." This kind of reward/punishment model gives children what they want if they comply and, although it may work temporarily, it's usually counterproductive in the long run.

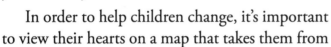

> Parents who don't embrace a good strategy often use what we call "Reactive Parenting."

Dora realized that she did more reacting to her daughter than was helpful. She would take away a privilege or yell at her when she did the wrong thing.

Dora was intrigued with the map idea and was eager to develop a strategy to help her daughter change.

There are many ways to get from point A to point B. The challenge is choosing the best path to get there. There's not just one right way to raise a child. You're trying to figure out what's best for your child. Some parents themselves are self-focused, coming up with their parenting ideas from their own past or from the latest book they've read. Unfortunately, many kids don't seem to respond to the typical approaches that these parents use. It's better to be child-focused when developing the plan. By "child-focused" we don't mean that we give kids whatever they want. Rather, we study a child to try to understand that child's heart. When we do, we often come up with strategies that are best for that child.

We're all changing, some for the better and others for the worse. If children aren't trained and are left to their own solutions in life, most of the time they find themselves moving in the wrong direction. That's not always true. Some kids are self-motivated to move forward toward maturity and responsibility, but most kids need training to guide their hearts to grow in the right direction.

Philippians 1:6 is just one of many verses in the Bible that provides hope for us that we are growing as God continues the change process in our lives. "Being confident of this, that he who began a good work in you will carry it on to completion until the day of Christ Jesus." God is growing each of us every day.

Parents are an important part of that growth in a child's life. Before we continue with more strategies and plans, let's examine the process of change a bit more in depth.

God is in the Business of Change

When a person comes to Christ and makes a personal decision to accept Jesus into his heart, then God begins to move that person from point A to point B. That process is called sanctification or spiritual growth. We're becoming more like Christ and eventually will see him face to face. That process of change takes place over our whole lifetime and accelerates at a rate that depends on our responsiveness to God's leadership.

As we work with children, we want to use many of the same heart-based strategies that God uses with us. As we do, we're likely to see change begin to take place relatively quickly. That doesn't mean that an emotional child will instantly become more self-controlled, or that a mean child will become compassionate overnight. But you should see progress toward the goal. As you work the plan, you position yourself and your child under God's grace, and he does the changing. The key is to develop a plan that meets the specific needs of your child.

> The key is to develop a plan that meets the specific needs of your child.

Dora studied her daughter, spent time praying, and then met with Sara to discuss the solutions. She explained it this way. "Sara, one of the things I want to help us develop in our family this year is the ability to think of others. I want to look for ways to bless others outside our home. I was thinking that we could look for one way each week to be of help to someone."

Dora knew that Sara would like this idea because she tended to like helping others outside the family. As they discussed it, Sara had some good ideas of things they could do. Dora knew that she was on the right track. In fact, Sara had heard at church about a woman who couldn't pay her phone bill. So, Mom helped Sara organize a few of her friends to do some extra work to earn money, and then they all went over to the woman's house and blessed her with the money to pay the bill. It was a sweet and rewarding time for all, especially Sara who led it.

Mom then brought the idea back to their own family. "I like what we did by showing love with the phone bill. That was a lot of fun. I was thinking also that we could work on it in our home somehow. If we could work as a team, I think it would strengthen our relationship, as well." Dora could see that this idea needed some time to sink in, so she stopped the dialogue for now. But later, when she asked Sara to stop playing and help clean up the floor, she got that same resistance that had developed into a pattern in their home. Dora stopped, paused for a moment to gain her composure, and decided to take a different route than she had in the past.

Dora sat down at the dining room table and said, "Sara, would you please come over here?" She didn't respond right away. "Sara, I'd like to talk to you. Please come over to the table."

Sara came over, sat down, and said with a rather grumpy voice. "What?"

"Hmm. I'm trying to figure out how to respond here. I want to have a cooperative relationship with you, but I feel like you're not working with me here. Can you change your attitude, or do I have to discipline you? I want you to sit here and think about your attitude for a few minutes and come to me when you're ready to work together with me."

> Remember that parents can't force a change of heart. However, they can have a powerful impact on the process.

Sara sat for about ten minutes, and Dora wondered what would happen next. Surprisingly, when Sara came over to Mom, her attitude had changed and she seemed ready to cooperate. Dora was encouraged.

Sara has a long way to go. Dora knows that, but she is changing the pattern of Sara being self-focused. It's going to take work, but Dora has some new strategies and techniques to help her daughter change.

Remember that parents can't force a change of heart. However, they can have a powerful impact on the process. Consider this example. When a child has a broken leg and goes to the doctor, the physician sets the bone and applies a cast. This allows the bone to heal properly. The doctor doesn't do the healing; God does. In a similar way, parents can create the cast for a child's heart so that God can do the healing necessary. The task you have as a parent is to know how best to create the cast.

If your child has a problem with meanness, lying, disrespect, or defiance, then your child needs therapy. And you're the best therapist for your child, if you have a good plan. The word "therapy" implies practice sessions. If a child can't walk, then the child gets physical therapy. If a child can't talk, then the solution involves speech therapy. In the same way, a child with a character deficiency needs character therapy, and you are a large part of the solution.

A good plan gathers the necessary tools to encourage change. If you have more than one child, then the plan will be different for each one. Every specific child's plan will connect with that child in order to move from point A to point B, hopefully with cooperation, but that's a luxury not always present in the change process.

Internal Motivation

As you develop your plan, you'll get further if you rely on internal motivation to empower your child toward point B. Internal motivation comes from the heart, but just because something comes from the heart, doesn't mean that it's good. Your son may be angry with his sister and punch her for taking his iPod. That's internal motivation, but it's not right. That's why God placed two things inside the human heart to keep it going in the right direction: the conscience and the Holy Spirit.

Together they provide an internal guidance system for the heart to keep it on track. As you develop your strategies in the coming chapters, look for ones that focus most directly on building internal motivation. That's where lasting change takes place. We'll embrace the conscience and the Holy Spirit in many of our suggestions. As you work along with what God is already doing in your child, then great things can happen.[5]

There are several significant tools that parents need in order to motivate change in a child's life. One of the tools that makes all the difference between success and failure is when parents transfer responsibility for change to the child.

Transferring Responsibility to the Child

One of the key pillars in a heart-based approach is to transfer responsibility

---

[5] A more complete study of internal motivation is presented in the book *Motivate Your Child: A Christian Parent's Guide to Raising Kids Who Do What They Need to Do Without Being Told.*

to the child. You'll see this one idea expanded and illustrated several times in this book. Let's start by choosing the words you might use that can imply that the problem belongs to your child. By choosing your words carefully, you can help your child see that he needs to work on his problem.

> One of the key pillars in a heart-based approach is to transfer responsibility to the child.

Something that led to success with Sara is that Dora helped her see that she could be part of the solution. Dora looked for ways to identify Sara's initiative, both good and bad, so that she could help her daughter see that this was an area of growth that would help her in her own life.

Here's a Bible story you might tell your child, found in John 5. A man, who had been lame for thirty-eight years, was sitting with other sick people near a pool in Jerusalem. Jesus came up to the man and asked him, 'Do you want to get well?' Why do you think Jesus would ask a man who was lame for that long if he wanted to get well? I think it's because some people like being sick. After all, if this guy got well, then he'd probably have to get a job, clean up his own messes, and cook his own food. Life would have to change. Jesus asked the question to make sure that the man actually wanted healing.

You might say to your child, "So, son, I see that you have a problem with _____. Do you want to get well?" You might find that your child doesn't particularly want to get well. That will likely affect your plan a bit, but it won't hinder your determination to move forward.

You'll want to evaluate the words you use when talking about your child's problem and look for ways to transfer the responsibility. For example, one mom continually used the words "I need you to…" with her uncooperative son. One of the ways she chose to turn this around was to say, "You need to…" Now the issue wasn't focused on Mom's needs but rather on the child's responsibility.

Here are some other phrases that might be helpful:

"Honey, I have an idea that might help you with your tendency to get angry."

"Bill, you did better today practicing cooperation. I'm impressed."

"Karen, I know that you're working on responding better to authority. This is an example of when you can practice."

"Son, it looks like you had a hard time managing your energy at school today, and it got you into trouble."

Each of these statements carefully addresses the issue as the child's problem but still offers hope for a solution. What are some things you might say to your child that would help imply that the problem belongs to your child and requires change in order to see progress?

The report card on the next page can help you evaluate the strength of your child's conscience.

Identifying Conscience Prompters

The conscience prompts a child in four areas: 1. Do what's right, 2. Deal with wrongs, 3. Be honest, and 4. Care about others. Take a few minutes and evaluate your child's conscience.[6]

Already Strong	Needs Improvement	**Do What's Right**
O	O	My child does what I say without resistance.
O	O	My child completes a job instead of doing it part way.
O	O	My child does what's right even when no one is around to watch.
O	O	My child is able to stand up against peer pressure.
O	O	My child works hard to complete a job that's difficult.
O	O	My child takes a stand for what's right.
O	O	My child reports back when a job is completed.
O	O	_____
O	O	_____

		Deal with Wrongs
O	O	My child admits when he's done the wrong thing.
O	O	My child responds well to correction.
O	O	My child values correction and learns from it.
O	O	My child accepts responsibility for his part of the problem.
O	O	My child feels remorse for an offense.
O	O	My child takes initiative to make wrongs right.
O	O	My child feels uncomfortable with wrong and seeks to avoid it.
O	O	_____
O	O	_____

---

[6] You might want to read Chapter 3 in **Motivate Your Child: A Christian Parent's Guide to Raising Kids Who Do What They Need to Do Without Being Told** to learn more about how the conscience prompts children in four areas and ways that you can increase that conscience awareness for your child.

Already Strong	Needs Improvement	**Be Honest**
O	O	My child tells the truth.
O	O	My child is honest when no one is watching.
O	O	My child avoids stealing, cheating, and lying.
O	O	My child speaks honestly when confronted with an offense.
O	O	My child takes a stand for integrity when faced with dishonest options.
O	O	My child tells a story without exaggerating or embellishing it.
O	O	_____
O	O	_____

		Care About Others
O	O	My child thinks about the feelings of others.
O	O	My child is kind to siblings, friends, and others.
O	O	My child is on the look out to help people.
O	O	My child cleans up his messes and contributes to the clean up of others too.
O	O	My child looks for things that need to be done and does them.
O	O	My child wants to make the world a better place.
O	O	_____
O	O	_____

You may find it easier to identify areas of weakness, but for your plan, you want to point out positive examples. Often, a child has strength in one area of the conscience while still having challenges in other areas. By pointing out your child's strengths, you'll raise the awareness level of promptings in the areas of weakness, as well.

When you draw attention to the conscience, you'll want to have some specific illustrations of how your child is already responding to internal prompters. Here are some examples:

"I noticed that you brought the trash can in from the curb without being asked."

"You managed your time well this morning instead of relying on me to get you out the door."

"When you offended your brother, you responded well to him by apologizing."

"You are quite strong in the honesty department of your life. It's a statement about who you are in your heart."

"What you did was thoughtful. You have some promptings in your heart that you're paying attention to that help you think about others. Good job!"

Give some examples here where your child responded to internal prompters instead of relying on external ones.

What part of the conscience is your child strongest in?

O Doing what's right

O Dealing with wrongs

O Being honest

O Caring about others

It would be helpful if you could think of a specific example that you might later share with your child. What is a positive example of your child responding to an internal prompting in at least one of the areas above?

_____

_____

_____

_____

_____

What area of your child's conscience do you think needs the most work?

O Doing what's right

O Dealing with wrongs

O Being honest

O Caring about others

We'll use this information more later on. For now, you're just preparing yourself for discussions you'll likely want to have with your child.

Have a Meeting with Your Child

The purpose of this meeting is to raise the awareness of the conscience. This discussion may take place in more than one setting, and might be best to have spontaneously. However, some children respond better to a formal sit-down meeting.

The conscience prompts you to be internally motivated.

First, you might draw a picture of a heart and say something like this: "Inside your heart you have a lot of things competing for your attention. Whatever wins then comes out in behavior. Here's what I mean.

"Do you ever get promptings in your heart to do something? (Here's where you might point out some of your positive observations of your child from the exercise above.) I noticed that the other day you went over and comforted our friend's baby without being asked. Was that the conscience or the Holy Spirit prompting you to do that? (Of course, most children, and even adults, have a hard time distinguishing between the conscience's and the Holy Spirit's promptings.) I'm not sure myself sometimes whether it's the conscience or the Holy Spirit, but the important thing is that you are aware of those internal promptings. God uses both of them to keep you going in the right direction.

"Let me explain more about what the conscience is. I think you'll find this very interesting. The conscience prompts you in four areas of your life. (Now, you might draw a circle with four sections, each one identified as a prompter of the conscience.)

"The conscience prompts you to be internally motivated. That's when you respond to the internal promptings and don't have to rely on external motivation to get things done. For example, in the morning, as you're getting ready for your day, if you rely on me to tell you to get dressed, make your bed, put your breakfast dishes away, comb your hair, and get your backpack, then you're relying on external prompters. But if you do those things on your own by keeping track of your to-do list, watching the clock, and prompting yourself, then that's internal motivation.

"Let me ask you a question. When I ask you to do something, why do you do what's right?"

Some children may say, "So I don't get in trouble."

You could respond, "Let's look at Romans 13:5 for a better understanding of internal and external motivation. It says, 'Therefore, it is necessary to submit to the authorities (do what you're asked to do), not only because of possible punishment (external motivation) but also as a matter of conscience (internal motivation).' That's interesting. As you grow and develop, you're going to learn to rely more heavily on internal motivation than external motivation, and I want to help you do that."

As you continue the dialogue, ask this question, "Does God speak to you?" Many children take this question to mean an audible voice, so they answer "No." But here, again, is an opportunity to raise the awareness level. You might say, "He speaks to me, and he may also be trying to speak to you. Sometimes he speaks through the Bible, sometimes he speaks through a person, and sometimes he speaks inside your heart."

Over the next few days, develop the idea of internal motivation by pointing out mostly positive examples of it in your child, yourself, and others. Occasionally, you might make reference to internal motivation in a correction situation, but be careful that you don't overemphasize the negative side of either the Holy Spirit's work or the conscience. Although those negative pieces are important, training is often needed in a child's heart in order to receive those promptings without resulting in self-condemnation, blaming, or other issues.

How did your meeting go? What did you learn? What worked?

_____

_____

_____

_____

_____

_____

_____

_____

_____

4

Working Together

If you truly want to understand your child, initiate change, watch the response, then pause and evaluate what's in the heart.

"I feel like my parenting is damaging my relationship with my son," said one dad. Most of us can identify with that feeling because the job of being a parent requires that we set limits, correct kids, and give them instructions regularly throughout the day. Those responsibilities often take an emotional toll on relationships. It just happens. It's as if a small amount of currency is withdrawn from the relational bank account each time we do the business of parenting—and it happens daily and even hourly or more at times.

> Kids often need parental discipline in order to build self-discipline.

In order for relationship to remain strong between a parent and a child, there must be a continual flow of deposits to balance out the withdrawals. On top of that reality, when a child has a particularly challenging tendency, then the continual discipline and training must be accompanied by regular doses of relational connectedness in order to maximize the change.

Some parents, to overcome the relational tension they experience, try to back off on the pressure. Sometimes that's necessary, but more often, the child needs the pressure in order to change. Therefore, the solution is to look for ways to keep up an appropriate amount of pressure while also strengthening the relationship. Firmness teaches character. Kids often need parental discipline in order to build self-discipline. A lax approach to parenting in order to preserve the relationship can often backfire because children need the structure and guidance provided by parents in order to overcome their weaknesses.[7]

It's important to remember that kids can only take as much pressure as the relationship allows. We work with tough cases where children have significant weaknesses requiring strategic action on the part of parents. We often tell parents that the plan is going to put pressure on the child, so it's important to increase relational connectedness at the same time.

---

[7]Chapter 13 in *Motivate Your Child: A Christian Parent's Guide to Raising Kids Who Do What They Need to Do Without Being Told* provides additional practical tips on building relationships with kids, even if they don't seem to respond well to your initiative.

Here's why. If your child has a significant weakness, then the interaction has likely taken a toll on your relationship already. A lack of closeness in the relationship increases resistance and frustration. That tension makes the process of training even more difficult, and a negative cycle often takes hold. The solution, then, is to build into your plan ways to meet relational needs while

at the same time strategically move a child toward the goal.

Sandra said it this way. "I can see a direct correlation between my daughter's acting out and decreased relational time between her and me. When I spend the time to rub her back before bed, laugh with her during the day, talk to her while she's eating a snack, and have significant conversations, she feels a sense of connection. Then, when she needs correction, she seems more willing to listen. I think when she feels loved and understood, she is less defensive and thus tends to be more responsive to me."

Another mom said, "My son resists relationships, and my attempts are often rejected." And it is true that negative patterns can form walls of resistance over time that make emotionally connecting difficult. But even the hardest heart can change. The key is knowing how to open those windows into a child's heart, and then discover ways to increase the warmth and light that flow through them. Relationship communicates that you care. That care often meets a need inside the child that prompts internal motivation to improve and change.

Let's divide the relationship building tools into two categories: Foundational and Supplemental. Foundational tools are proactive, looking for general ways to connect with a child's heart. Supplemental tools accompany your instructions, correction, and limit-setting. They make your words and actions more palatable.

Foundational Tools for Building a Stronger Relationship

If your relationship with your child is strong and you experience closeness on a regular basis, be grateful and continue to invest in the relationship as you develop a plan for change. If your relationship is a struggle and often threatened, be sure to think through this part of the plan very carefully. A close relationship gives you greater opportunities to reach a child's heart.

> If your relationship is a struggle and often threatened, be sure to think through this part of the plan very carefully.

It's interesting to discover what kinds of things contribute to a stronger relationship with each child. Sometimes it's common activities. Other times it's significant conversations. It may be physical touch or acts of kindness. In any case, building relationships requires thoughtfulness. Take a moment and ask yourself the question, "What kinds of things can I do that contribute to a close relationship between me and my child?" Write a few answers here:

_____

_____

_____

_____

The more challenging a child is, the more difficult it is for a parent to reach out in ways that connect relationally. One mom said, "When my son fights me at every turn and treats me with disrespect, it hurts me a lot. It's hard to think about building a stronger relationship. I don't even feel like talking to him sometimes."

That mom's honest words mimic the hearts of many parents. It's in those moments that the only way to parent effectively is to draw on the strength provided by God in your heart. Imagine that you are the counselor for a moment and counsel yourself to finish these sentences.

When I feel like withdrawing, I need to say to myself...

_____

_____.

When I don't feel like initiating pleasant conversation with my child, I need to remember _____

_____.

The relational side of parenting is not optional. If you're going to move your child from point A to point B, relationship is often the vehicle that allows you to pass on key ideas and relevant truths.

Sometimes the tactics parents use to build relationships don't seem to directly correlate to the problem the child has, yet the strengthened relationship somehow affects the problem in positive ways.

> The relational side of parenting is not optional.

Janene told us about her daughter, Becky. "I have a challenging six-year-old. She gets angry when she makes mistakes. She has meltdowns at soccer when she misses a ball, and when she plays board games, she has to win or it's a crisis. She often quits things when she gets frustrated, then she sulks and complains."

We told Janene that, before we start working on a specific plan for anger management, she should first build some underlying relationship with her daughter. She decided that she would intentionally show love to her daughter three times a day. "I determined to give her a gift of my attention, since I sensed that would minister most to her heart. I worked ahead in my own schedule so that I could take extra time with her. Some of our love times were spontaneous when she wanted to tell me a story or needed comfort for some disappointment, but I had to plan most of the love gifts. I sometimes sat with her at breakfast in the morning, planned riddles and kid jokes to share at random times, and I spent extra time tucking her in at night. We connected around afternoon snack and in the evening."

Janene began to see some changes even before we implemented the anger management plan with her daughter. "She seemed more relaxed and was willing to respond to my care when she started to get overwhelmed with anger. I would sometimes hug her when she got angry, something I hadn't done before. I think she responded well to the rest of my strategies because we had these love times together."

Janene was successful with her daughter in part because she valued the relationship and demonstrated that value intentionally. Building relational bonds with a child creates an atmosphere that makes change easier and more effective. Look for ways to build a strong foundation with a relationship on which you'll build the rest of your plan.

Supplemental Tools for Maintaining a Strong Relationship

Often, the parents' approach prompts a predictable, negative response. Things like yelling, interrupting, nagging, or barging into a child's space, can set them off and increase resistance and defensiveness. On the other hand, supplementing your firmness with more relational strategies can make all the difference.

This is an area of wisdom and may require the development of new skills. Those parents who act based on the fact that they are right and the child is wrong sometimes justify all kinds of relationship draining techniques. It was interesting for me (Scott) to work with Richard, a dad of a challenging fifteen-year-old son we'll call Jason.

When I challenged Richard about his harshness with Jason, he responded, "But he won't listen. He's continually sarcastic and treats me like dirt." Do you see what Richard did? He justified his poor treatment of Jason because his son was wrong. A wise parent will not only see that the child is wrong but will also look for techniques to accompany the necessary correction that will maximize change. The goal isn't revenge. The goal is change.

I shared with Richard a verse from the Bible. "First Peter 4:8 says, 'Above all, love each other deeply, because love covers over a multitude of sins.'" I continued, "The love that you show to Jason will help ease the frustrations in the relationship. Sometimes the sin is on the part of the child, and sometimes it's on the part of the parent. All sins need to be addressed at the right time with the right approach. However, in the end, both parents and children are imperfect people. We all need the grace of God in our lives. We're all weak. We need humility to change ourselves, perseverance to work on tough problems in our kids, and love to keep relationships strong."

Richard realized that he was taking Jason's sarcasm too personally. Yes, it's hard not to take personally some of the disrespect and selfishness our kids dish out. But it's best to keep the problem the child's problem and, using a number of strategies, move that child to where he needs to be.

Wise parents use supplemental tools to strengthen relationship when they need to correct, set limits, and give instructions. That wisdom often involves gentleness, respecting the child, calmness, listening, and patience, all skills that encourage relational connectedness.

> We all need the grace of God in our lives.

Richard was impressed with the changes he saw in Jason as he continued to work hard on his approach. It took him a while to find some things that worked with Jason. I encouraged him to ask his son what things he could do to improve the relationship. Just asking the question seemed to increase a positive dynamic. It was as if Dad was saying to his son, "Let's work together. I want to have a better relationship with you, and I'm willing to change."

Jason, seeing his dad's desire, responded quite well. Jason suggested that his dad not yell at him. Dad agreed to work on that. In fact, he determined to correct in a whisper to show that he was working on it. Jason paid attention more and became more responsive to his father. When Jason started being mean, Dad just quietly walked out instead of his former approach of overpowering his son. A few minutes later, he gently came back and said, "Could we try that again?" Jason got the message and, over time, became less defensive and more responsive to his dad.

In addition, Richard realized that his correction of his son was received better when he started with a question instead of a statement. "Can you help me here? I'm feeling like you're not responding to me about the dishes. I asked you fifteen minutes ago to help in the kitchen, and I don't see you moving. I'm not quite sure what's going on." He was surprised at the positive response that came from his son. "Oh, yeah, I'll do it now," and he did. It was amazing to see the change between Richard and Jason when Dad chose to emphasize relationship as part of his action plan.

What are some things you could do to make your limits, instructions, or corrections more relational?

_____

_____

_____

_____

_____

_____

Sometimes a relational approach is all that's needed to increase cooperation and decrease resistance. When parents are willing to reach out their hand in relationship, some children quickly respond in kind. However, some children need more than just relationship building. In fact, there are five tools that will help move your child from point A to point B.

But don't be too quick to move to the next several chapters. Instead, spend some extra time here. Study your child. Look for ways to strengthen relationship, both foundationally and supplementally. It's amazing how much your work in this area will pay off. It'll be well worth your time and energy.

> When parents are willing to reach out their hand in relationship, many children quickly respond in kind.

Have a Meeting with Your Child

You'll likely have relationship meetings quite regularly with your child. Other meetings will define the problem and develop a strategic plan, but this meeting emphasizes relationship. It's most important that you choose a time that isn't in the midst of discipline.

Sometimes the meeting is just for strengthening the relationship without any other agenda. You'll simply be looking for ways to connect about common experiences, likes and dislikes, or understanding some of the opinions your child might have.

Either way, the purpose of this meeting is to connect with your child's heart. With an older child you may go out to a local coffee shop to sit and talk. Maybe you'll take your child out for breakfast or ice cream or go for a walk together. Ideally, you'll do something that your child enjoys doing that also allows you the

opportunity to talk. There's no particular topic or agenda. Mostly, you want to be available to listen, but you may need to do some sharing to get the ball rolling.

Your goal is to connect and to feel just a little closer to each other's hearts than you did before the meeting, so be sure not to bring your lectures or criticisms to this meeting, just your vulnerability and time.

How did your meeting go? What did you learn? What worked?

_____

_____

_____

_____

_____

_____

_____

_____

_____

5

A Place for Firmness

The path from a caterpillar to a butterfly requires struggle.

The design of a human is fascinating. The more you study medicine, the more you become awestruck by the intricate workings of the human body. When it comes to the way a person makes choices, experiences emotions, and develops a lifestyle, the process is equally as intriguing. The complexity is seen most clearly when someone wants to change. Desires, emotions, beliefs, passions, and convictions all collide in the heart. As you continue to learn more about the heart, the process of change will make more sense.

But what prompts that change? Most people decide to make changes in their lives for one or both of two reasons. First, because of new information, insight, or a vision for something better. Or second, because of discomfort with the present situation.

> As you continue to learn more about the heart, the process of change will make more sense.

When an adult decides to change jobs, it's typically because either she hears about a different job with better pay, a more pleasant commute, or a more desired job description; or she simply is so dissatisfied with her current job that she needs a change. These same two factors are at work when you move to a new home, change your diet, or simply buy some new clothes. You see the benefits of something different or no longer want to be where you are. You then move from point A to point B.

When helping a child change, you'll want to take advantage of these same two factors to motivate and empower the change process. The action plan for change involves five components. As you develop a written action plan, the first component is Firmness. Firmness makes point A uncomfortable. We will walk you through all five components, but in this chapter, we'll devote ourselves to understanding how firmness creates motivation to change and how to add appropriate firmness to your action plan.

Remember, the goal of parenting isn't just to make kids happy. Those whose primary goal to make their children feel good often raise selfish children. Kids need firmness in order to move away from their weaknesses. Many kids are very comfortable with laziness, emotional outbursts, or disrespect. They need loving parents who are willing to set firm boundaries to help them move forward toward the goal of maturity.

Mindy was concerned about her twelve-year-old son, Mark. He played video games every waking moment he could. He obviously loved the games, but Mom knew something needed to change. We asked her, "Why is it a problem that your son spends so much time playing video games?"

"I feel like he's missing out. I wish he would be creative, spend time with friends, or help out around the house."

Firmness makes point A uncomfortable.

"Great. Those are good ideas. It's best if you have some positive choices in your plan and not just tell him what he needs to stop doing. Here's an idea. Maybe you could limit the video game time to one or two hours a day and require that he come up with some alternatives of things that he could do instead. Mark could report to you what he's done toward building relationships, helping out at home, or engaging in some kind of creativity. In fact, maybe his gaming time could be earned by making progress in these other areas."

Mom liked that idea but anticipated a battle. "He's not going to like this."

"You're right. You'll likely experience resistance. But, remember, your goal isn't to make Mark happy. Your goal is to change how he uses his time. Let's look for the best way to present this plan, share the concern, and involve him in the process. Then, you'll need to make sure this is something that's important enough to you as a mom and that you're ready to do the hard work required to help Mark make changes in his life."

Mindy was ready. She knew change needed to take place, and this more positive approach, that contained alternatives and a mindset for moving forward, was just what they needed. The next week, she reported back. Mark was angry at first, but Mom had been calm and, after a couple of days, when he saw that his mom meant it and wasn't just complaining, he knew he had to make adjustments. It wasn't easy, but in only a week, Mindy was seeing changes in her son.

Character Develops Under Pressure

Challenges and difficulties build perseverance, thoughtfulness, patience, and humility. Paul confirmed that in the Bible when he wrote these words, "suffering produces perseverance; perseverance, character; and character, hope."

> Firmness simply makes it clear that life will be a particular way.

(Romans 5:3-4) Too often parents either rescue their children from the challenges of life or try to avoid difficulties, but kids need those tough times to help them develop character.

When children acquire an entitlement mentality, demonstrate a bad attitude about helping out in simple tasks around the house, or react with anger when things don't go the way they'd like, it's a sign that some heart work is necessary. Those tendencies come from the innermost center of a person's being and are a demonstration of a lack of character in one area or another.

Firmness helps draw a line inside a child's heart, defining right from wrong, what's appropriate and what's not appropriate. The conscience needs training, and firmness clarifies the basis upon which the conscience draws its information.

But what is firmness, and how can we get the most out of this piece of the strategy? Firmness simply makes it clear that life will be a particular way. It's not optional. Sometimes all that's needed is an authoritative stand. Other times a consequence may prompt change. The point is that parental leadership guides the child from a negative place to a more healthy or responsible way to live.[8]

---

[8] You might want to read Chapter 9 in *Motivate Your Child: A Christian Parent's Guide to Raising Kids Who Do What They Need to Do Without Being Told* to learn more ideas about making consequences work effectively in your plan. You'll also discover several types of consequences for your toolbox.

Christina said it this way. "My three girls, ages eight, six, and four, often have a hard time getting along. Sometimes two of them pair up and leave the other one crying because she feels left out. Friction often builds with name-calling, yelling, and physical roughness. When I step in and insist on better problem-solving techniques and kindness, they respond, but they seem to need me to remind them. The girls require me to be firm at times, because they aren't yet ready to manage their own selfishness. I'm trying to work with each of them independently, but until I see more self-control, I realize I need to use parental control to help them."

Kids often need firmness to motivate them toward new habits. When parents hear the word "firmness," they often think in terms of consequences. Although consequences are important, firmness is broader than that. It means saying no when appropriate and sticking to it. It means following through when you give an instruction to make sure the child completes the task.

Don't confuse firmness with harshness. Firmness draws a line that says, "This is not optional." Harshness adds emotional intensity to show that you mean business. Harshness damages the relationship and isn't necessary. Some parents say, "My kids don't start moving unless I start yelling." If that's true, it's because you've trained them that way. By tightening your action point, the point where you stop talking and start acting, you can retrain your kids to respond to instructions without the need to yell.

Pause for a moment and consider your action point. Ask yourself this question, "How do my kids know when I mean business and that they better start moving right away? What cues do I give to them that they better act now?"

_____

_____

_____

Then ask your child this question, "When I've given you an instruction, how do you know when you better start moving? What cues do I give to you that indicate I'm serious?" If they need help, you might say, "Some kids say their parents have a certain look, or they do something with their voice. What do you think?" Write the answers here.

_____

_____

_____

It's surprising what we can learn from our kids about our own interactions. In fact, sometimes the above conversation with your child will lead you to make some adjustments. Parents can fall into patterns and assume that kids should just respond. Often, a small adjustment in the way an instruction is presented can foster more cooperation.

Firmness often means following through, saying no, or being clear and refusing to budge, and, yes, sometimes firmness does involve consequences. Some children need consequences in order for their hearts to choose to live differently. The purpose of consequences, however, is not justice—you did this, so you deserve that. The purpose of a consequence is to make point A uncomfortable in order to motivate the child to change. Consequences can be used to get the child's attention, to say, "This is important."

Molly told us this story. "My son, age twelve, has a problem with back-talk. It just seems to flow out of his mouth. In the past, I've taken his iPad away for a day or a week as a consequence, but it doesn't seem to help. So, instead of setting a time, I chose to tell him that he could have his iPad back when he earned it, by showing me that he was working on the problem and becoming more respectful. He just looked at me, thought for a moment, and then said, 'How am I supposed to do that?'

"I then realized that I was doing more complaining about the problem than I was working toward a solution. So, we started to make some adjustments. At first, any changes he made were small. In fact, sometimes he pointed to ways he was changing that seemed quite insignificant to me. I affirmed him for those but tried to help him understand that this was a much bigger problem.

"There was one particular conversation that seemed to make the difference. I sat down with him one evening and told him that the problem of back-talk was hurting our relationship and that taking away the iPad was part of helping him see that. In fact, at the rate of change we were seeing, he probably wouldn't get his iPad back for a year. His mouth dropped and his eyes opened wide. After the shock wore off, we had an opportunity to discuss the issue. He said, 'That's a big punishment. I think it's too big.' I replied, 'I think the back-talk is a big problem.' He got the idea, because from that point, I started seeing him try harder and make significant progress."

What are some examples of consequences that you tend to use with your child?

Sometimes, a conversation with your child about consequences can lead to some new solutions. "Son, I'd like to work with you to figure out a good response when I think you need a consequence. I'm open to ideas from you. The goal is to address negative patterns that you have in your heart, and I think that a consequence might be a good first step. But maybe you have a better idea. What are your thoughts?"

> Sometimes, a conversation with your child about consequences can lead to some new solutions.

You might want to pose a particular example and allow your child to give you some suggestions about your parenting. Openness at this level can be helpful because it reveals that you're real and willing to work on the relationship together while, at the same time, doing your job as a parent. It's interesting to watch children become more responsive when parents invite them to be part of the solution.

Firmness is important because it says, "We can't continue to live this way anymore." When parents come to that conclusion personally, then they're often ready for a plan to move forward. Of course, some parents aren't ready to change. Either they don't see the problem developing yet, or they don't have the energy or ideas required to do the necessary work. Looking for ways to identify problems early in your child's life will help you offset tendencies, address the heart, and head off a major issue. We're not suggesting that you become paranoid about your child's future, but recognizing indicators of negative trends can help you take action earlier.

Responding to a Crisis

In some cases, problems accumulate for a time and then eventually erupt into a crisis. That crisis then increases the readiness a reluctant parent might have to mandate change. Most parents second-guess themselves, often wondering if they are being too strict or too lenient. That's usually a good thing and helps parents be sensitive to the specific needs of their family. But sometimes parents become numb to the growing problems because of the daily work of parenting. Then comes a crisis, and a parent realizes that change is required.

If you have kids, you'll have crises. They come. It's part of being a parent. The question is, will you be ready to respond in the best way to the next crisis, or will you just react and express your displeasure? The crisis might be a poor report from school, discovering something in your child's backpack, seeing something troubling in your computer's Internet history, or even a visit from the police to your home. Often, these kinds of events motivate a parent to concentrate on a specific area of life more. A crisis is always an opportunity to make significant changes. Furthermore, the child is often more receptive in the midst of a crisis, recognizing that the parent has justification for a firm response.

> If you have kids, you'll have crises. They come. It's part of being a parent.

When the crisis takes place, remember these two things. First, it's an opportunity to change the rules. You may respond to the crisis by taking away a cell phone or choosing to park it overnight, changing the way homework is done, or checking up on a child more often. You might also use that crisis to change the schedule, require church or youth group attendance, or even require counseling.

The second thing to remember is that you'll get one significant conversation. Sometimes you get more, but you'll have at least one conversation where you'll be able to explain your concern, the dangers of the situation, and the plan to overcome this challenge. Don't waste that conversation by just yelling at a child. Plan it well.

When Charisa found out that her ten-year-old son, Michael, stole a baseball bat from another boy at school, she planned her response. Not only did she go with him to apologize to the coach and the student, but she also used the opportunity to tighten up some of the things going on at home. Instead of giving him freedom to play with his hand-held video game, she required that he complete certain tasks and get his work approved in order to earn that privilege. Mom knew that if her son was becoming more lax in his heart and willing to steal, then he needed self-discipline in his life in other ways.

Another way to use firmness is to increase accountability and monitoring of a child's actions. The goal is to either prevent poor choices or to catch those choices earlier. A teen may need a closer watch on computer activity. An elementary-age child might need supervision to turn in school assignments. And two kids who tend to fight might need to play in the same room as a parent in order for earlier intervention in sibling conflict.

It's this form of firmness that Judy used to help her three-year-old daughter, Emily, to address her biting problem. When Emily became overwhelmed with her anger, she would bite the closest person she could find. Usually, that meant another child was the target. Play dates were a continual problem, and Judy knew that she needed to do something about it.

She first gave her daughter an alternative. "When you get unhappy about something, you need to say, 'I don't like that,' instead of biting." It was a simple plan, but it needed lots of practice. Instead of removing her daughter from frustrating experiences, she monitored her play. Mom allowed Emily to play with LEGOs with her friend, but determined to stay close by for quick intervention if her daughter's frustration level got out of hand.

Judy saw changes because she worked the plan and was quick to act. She gave her daughter alternatives to biting and trained her to respond differently.

> Character can naturally wear away and give in to desires that weaken a person's integrity.

Firmness draws a person back to the basics and requires that kids turn their focus from all the activity and busyness of life to foundational qualities such as self-discipline, responsibility, honesty, and thoughtfulness of others. Those qualities don't tend to naturally take place in anyone's life. Firmness is often needed to build and grow them. Parents and kids can develop tendencies to drift away from what's best. Character can naturally wear away and give in to desires that weaken a person's integrity.

Take a moment and write down some ways you might use firmness to address a particular problem you're working on with your child now.

_____

_____

_____

_____

Have a Meeting with Your Child

One of the ways to communicate firmness to your child is with a meeting where you explain the problem you're seeing, listen to your child's suggestions, and explore possible solutions together. In the end, however, if your child doesn't want to cooperate, this meeting may simply define the problem and reveal changes that will take place.

Kids sometimes don't want to change. They're very comfortable where they are. But when parents change, then kids have to change, so, in this meeting, you may simply communicate the changes you'll be making.

Let's take a problem of the poor report from school. Maybe you had given your daughter some freedom to manage herself when it comes to homework, but you found out that the work isn't being completed and/or turned in. It's time to take some action. You've already had the conversation with your daughter about her solving the problem herself, but it doesn't seem to be working, so it's time to reveal the new plan.

You might say, "It looks like you're still having trouble getting your homework done and turned in on your own. Do you have any thoughts about why your current plan isn't working?"

It's important to listen to a child's plan, but the measure of whether it's working is determined by the reports coming from school, not by the student.

"We're going to change the way we work on this for a while. I'm setting up a plan to communicate with your teacher so that I know what the assignments are. I'm going to require you to work on homework when you come home from school and show it to me before you have screen time. There's a new folder in your backpack to use for work going to and from school so that you know what needs to be turned in." Let's see if you can get things turned in using this kind of organizational plan or if we need to add some more to this process. I'd rather not add a consequence for not turning in homework, but if we have to go there, that will be the next step. If this new method works for a while, there will be no consequence, and I'll be happy to pull back and let you manage it yourself again. For now, however, let's see if we can get things back on track and moving in the right direction."

There are many ways that firmness works itself out. When a parent gets more involved in a child's schoolwork, checks with the teacher, and asks questions of the child and the teacher, then the child is held more accountable. Yelling and harshness don't need to escalate the challenges. Simply taking more initiative, following up, asking more questions, and giving consequences when necessary communicates the message that things need to change.

How did your meeting go? What did you learn? What worked?

_____

_____

_____

_____

_____

_____

_____

_____

_____

6

Visioning Moves You Forward

Change often has hidden benefits. The problem is finding them.

As we stated in the previous chapter, people change for one or both of two reasons. Either they become uncomfortable with life the way it is (firmness creates this feeling), or they gain a vision for something better. So, now let's talk about vision. Kids need to know why they should change.

One mom said to her son, "I'm going to help you develop kindness toward your sister. You'll learn how to respond well when annoyed, but I'll also help you learn how to treat other people with love. As you grow in this area, you'll set yourself up to be a better friend to others, and you'll be preparing to be a

great dad and husband someday." Visioning is important for children and helps them know why you're helping them develop a particular character quality in life. Kids need to understand what the goal looks like, not just what they need to stop doing.

Look at Things from a Higher Perspective

The conscience doesn't simply prompt kids to avoid wrongs in life. It prompts kids to a higher calling, a vision for something better. In the Bible, it was a vision for something new or different that turned common people into heroes.

David had a vision for God's strength and was then able to conquer a giant. God used dreams to carry Joseph through some tough times and helped him stay committed to doing what's right. In the book of Daniel, when the three brave friends were faced with the choice of bowing to the image or being executed, they said, "If we are thrown into the blazing furnace, the God we serve is able to deliver us from it, and he will deliver us from Your Majesty's hand. But even if he does not, we want you to know, Your Majesty, that we will not serve your gods or

> In the Bible, it was a vision for something new or different that turned common people into heroes.

worship the image of gold you have set up." (Daniel 3:17-18)

Vision is powerful, but many kids live in the moment and don't think beyond their day-to-day interactions. Parents encourage the development of internal motivation when they help their children catch a vision for why the current changes contribute to the bigger picture.

Three levels of thinking illustrate how visioning works. Level 1 is simply thinking about the activity at hand, whether it be eating lunch, watching TV, or playing with a friend. Level 2 thinking asks other questions, such as: "What time is it?" "What else should I be doing?" "How do others feel right now?" and "Is my current activity the best thing for me to be doing at the moment?" Those are responsibility questions. Level 3 thinking considers what God is doing, what he desires of me right now, and where he's taking me in my life. The more we can move children toward Level 2 and Level 3 thinking, the more vision we'll help them embrace.[9]

In the same way that firmness makes a child feel uncomfortable about point A, visioning creates an attraction to point B. Keep in mind that some children are willing to change even without the firmness, because they have a vision for something better. The goal of parenting isn't to simply react to problems. Reactive parenting sees things that are wrong and responds to them. Heart work requires more strategy than that, and visioning is an important piece.

Kristen said it this way, "My parenting was always negative. I was continually saying 'No' and 'Stop that.' I felt like I was being critical, which is not like me. I needed something different. When I caught this idea about visioning, I knew that it would help me. I've now changed the way I work with my kids by focusing more on the solution than on the problem. I like myself better as a parent, and my kids have noticed the change as well."

---

[9] You might want to read Chapter 11 in the book *Motivate Your Child: A Christian Parent's Guide to Raising Kids Who Do What They Need to Do Without Being Told* to learn more about developing level three thinking. It's amazing what happens to kids when they start to see God at work around them.

Visioning Answers the Question "Why?"

When kids understand how the required change fits into the bigger plan of life, it often gives them a greater internal desire to change. And even if they aren't internally motivated to make those changes, your continual emphasis on the future will keep you focused on the goal, in hopes that they will come around.

Some parents are surprised to find that their kids are actually willing to change when they get a vision for why and how that change is beneficial. Many times, just changing the way you parent can open new doors for kids to grow and mature, and they become willing to walk through them. If kids don't change with a new vision, you can always add the firmness to provide additional motivation, but don't discount the value of simply providing new perspective on a typical problem to help kids move forward. Furthermore, if you need to rely heavily on firmness strategies, be sure to add doses of visioning along the way to help kids get a grasp for why the change is helpful.

Imagine developing a strategy for Corinne, a seven-year-old girl who said "no" to everything, no matter how it was presented to her. She was in the habit of saying "no" to her mom when given almost any kind of instruction. Her tendency was to react with a negative response. Mom's friends were saying that Corinne had Oppositional Defiant Disorder, and maybe she did. ODD is the tendency to resist, and the solution is training by practicing following instructions with a better response.

Mom realized that Corinne had a problem and determined to make some changes. She had some firmness ideas lined up, but she knew that just being firm tended to prompt Corinne to become more entrenched. She wanted to try a different approach and added visioning to the plan. Later in this chapter, we'll share some of the ideas we came up with and what actually worked with her, but first, let's explain a little bit more about this component of the plan.

Once you've identified the character quality to work on at point B and defined it in a way that makes sense for your child, then explaining why that quality is helpful for life is a strategic step. Here are some visioning kinds of statements:

"Bob, I'm going to help you work on your anger because developing self-control in this area of your life will equip you to be a better husband someday. You're almost thirteen years old, and this is a great time for you to learn how to manage your anger as you're entering the very important teen years. I know that angry people are unhappy people, so when you develop some of the skills I'm going to teach you, then you'll actually enjoy life more and be able to handle very tough situations. People will look to you for solutions, and you'll also be able to help your friends deal with their emotional challenges."

For some children, visioning is powerful and works on its own.

"Randi, I can see that you struggle with focusing in class. I understand your challenge in that area. It seems that several distractions tend to grab your attention. So, I'm going to help you work on focusing. It's going to require some determination on your part, but, as you work on this, you'll see amazing things happen inside your heart. The urges that you have to move away from the task at hand will be overcome with a determination to focus. Imagine what this will do for you. It's going to be great. Other people will get distracted by something, but you'll be able to stay the course. You'll get more done, and you'll get it done more quickly. Working on this quality in your life won't just help you do well in class, but it will also help you in other areas too. I know that you like to create things. Maybe God is helping you to become an inventor or an artist. Those people need to focus. Working on determination is going to be very helpful."

What Prompts Change Internally?

In parenting, it's strategic to take advantage of both firmness and visioning. You might read the visioning comments above and say to yourself, "That's not going to work with my child." And that may be true. For some children, visioning is powerful and works on its own. It's surprising what happens when kids are internally motivated to take action in a positive way. But some children have developed rather complicated patterns of resistance. Visioning is important,

Firmness is important, but visioning wins the day.

but it's only one of five components of a good plan. Kids often need the other four, including the firmness already discussed in the previous chapter.

However, it's important to realize that, as firmness begins to take effect, it's actually the visioning that provides hope and direction. Some parents feel discouraged because they've applied firmness heavily and it isn't working. Some kids need more than firmness in order to make a change. Firmness can motivate change, but kids have to have a vision for moving to something new, or they just become more accustomed to living an uncomfortable life. Firmness is important, but visioning wins the day.

Ask Yourself "Why?"

As an exercise, take a moment and think about visioning regarding a weakness a child has. First, we'll offer illustrations of other kids. Then, you can apply this to your own child. Write some reasons why it would be helpful for the following children to develop the character quality needed in their lives.

1. Kimberly tends to leave messes around the house. At fourteen years old, she is certainly capable of being more thoughtful. Share a vision for developing thoughtfulness in her life.

   _____

   _____

   _____

   _____

2. Jackson is eight years old and gets angry when he receives a "no" answer. He needs to develop flexibility to handle his disappointment. Why is this important?

_____

_____

_____

_____

_____

3. Cindy is defiant at age five. She needs to develop cooperation and responsiveness to authority. How will those qualities help her?

_____

_____

_____

_____

_____

In Corinne's case, Mom would like to see two qualities developed: responsiveness to authority and cooperation. Mom realized that she was using a rather negative approach with her daughter by confronting her and threatening her. So, Mom had a meeting with her daughter, described the problem in objective, non-inflammatory terms, and then talked about the danger of being defiant and the advantages of being cooperative. Mom offered to change the way she gave instructions, and Corinne's suggestion was that her mom not yell at her.

Mom felt like saying, "Yelling? I don't yell at you. If you want to hear yelling, I can show that to you." But instead, Mom said, "Okay, not yelling. I can work on that. How would you like me to respond instead?" Corinne asked that she use a quieter voice. Mom agreed to try that.

The thing that tied it all together for them, though, was this piece of visioning that Mom shared with her daughter. "I want to have a good relationship with you. It seems that, for some reason, sometimes you're irritated with the instructions I give you, and then you react by saying 'No.' That 'no' answer damages our relationship. It's not the right response, and it hurts me. I'm trying to have a good relationship with you. I'd like to see you work on that too. If we both developed it, then good things can happen between us."

That seemed to click for Corinne, and Mom was able to use a combination of firmness, a change in her voice, and a reminder about their relationship to start the process of changing Corinne's tendency.

In the problem you're working on in your family, write down some visioning ideas that you might be able to share. How will the character quality at point B be helpful for your child?

_____

_____

_____

_____

Have a Meeting with Your Child

You might want to announce this meeting with your child by setting the tone in a positive way, "Hey, _____. I've got some things to share with you that I think you'll find interesting. I've got some solutions for you that are going to make your life better. Let's plan to get together after dinner this evening, and I'll share my ideas and see what you think of them."

At the meeting, be sure to describe the problem in objective terms and do it in a way that points out the child's choices. For example, "I noticed that we have a problem with the bathroom. The counter is sometimes messy. I think you're pretty busy and sometimes don't remember to straighten it before you leave." The idea that "we" have a problem is helpful, but it's also valuable to address the issue by identifying the challenge that the child faces.

Earlier we talked about transferring responsibility to the child. It was then that we suggested that the word "you" might be helpful in the conversation. Is it best to use "we" or "you?" The answer to that question is determined by your goal. In this case, we're suggesting that "we" might increase a sense of teamwork. You'll have to decide which is best to use this time in your dialogue.

> Look for particular points in your visioning that will touch your child's heart.

As you share some of your visioning ideas, remember that kids are all unique. Some like to know how this quality will help them do better in the work world someday, especially if you tie it into the child's desired career. Others like to know that working on this quality is a sign of maturity or helps them now start acting like six years old or twelve years old, a year ahead of where they are right now. Others like to see how the new quality in their lives will help them be successful in life now or increase persuasiveness, reputation, or relationship. Look for particular points in your visioning that will touch your child's heart. This is one of the significant ways to consider your child's uniqueness and tie your action plan into specific needs and desires.

Visioning will keep your parenting positive and help you focus on the real meaning of discipline. Some people imagine that discipline simply means correction, but it's much more than that. The root of the word discipline means "to teach." Visioning is a very important part of keeping the focus on training your child for the future.

How did your meeting go? What did you learn? What worked?

_____

_____

_____

_____

_____

_____

_____

_____

_____

7

Teaching Shows the Way

Inspiration from someone else can spark a wildfire of change inside of us.

Ralph is ten years old and has a problem with impulsivity. He gets into trouble at his Christian school because he talks too much. Each day, the teacher gives out red cards to kids who disrupt class or disobey the rules. Ralph gets several cards a day. When Ralph's parents talk to him, he feels bad because he likes school, likes his teacher, loves the Lord, and wants to do the right thing. But he continues to accumulate red cards daily, resulting in various punishments.

Teaching Communicates "How"

Just as vision answers the question "why," teaching answers the question "how." The teaching component adds feet to your strategy and provides the traction necessary for progress to take place.

As I (Scott) began to work with Ralph, we identified three arenas where he tended to get into trouble. One was in class during transitions between subjects. The second was for talking in the hall on the way to lunch or recess. And the third was just being silly in class with other boys. As we talked together, Ralph developed a plan, with guidance from me and from his parents.

Ralph decided that, when the teacher flashed the lights, the signal to come to order in class, then Ralph would put his hand over his mouth, applying the verse from Proverbs 30:32, "If you've played the fool…clap your hand over your mouth." When walking to recess or lunch, he decided to develop a new habit of looking down at his feet from the time he left one door until the time he got to the next. And when his friends started to be silly, he determined to focus on the teacher, realizing he was in danger of being tempted. In each case, we identified the arena where the challenge took place and a plan to address the specific temptation.

> Just as vision answers the question "why," teaching answers the question "how."

Ralph is doing much better in school and, most days, he doesn't get any cards at all. What he needed was some teaching, not a deck of red cards.[10]

---

[10]You might want to read Chapter 10 in the book *Motivate Your Child: A Christian Parent's Guide to Raising Kids Who Do What They Need to Do Without Being Told* for ideas of ways to teach kids how to handle specific life situations.

Actually, the red cards weren't the problem. Some kind of indicator, like a card, can be helpful, but that approach alone is incomplete. Cards represent the firmness component of the plan. But children often need more than firmness in order to change the tendencies of their hearts. I not only gave Ralph a vision for something better, but I also helped him develop a plan to do it. The most effective strategy for change is to work on the heart, not just the behavior. This involves more than pointing out a weakness. A good plan often requires a multifaceted approach. Teaching is a key component.

The red card program used in this school is an example of behavior modification. You get a bad thing when you do a bad thing, and you get a good thing if you do a good thing. In correction, it focuses on the wrong action. Behavior modification places a heavy emphasis on guilt as a motivator. Guilt itself isn't a bad emotion, but, if significant change needs to take place, kids need plans and training, not guilt trips. They need to know where they're going and how they're going to get there. The book of Proverbs gives special emphasis to the idea of training children. Proverbs 22:6 says, "Train up a child in the way he should go; even when he is old he will not depart from it." (ESV) Placing more emphasis on training instead of simply pointing out a weakness results in a greater ability to change.

> When a habit develops, it bypasses the decision-making center of the brain.

Some of the acting out that Ralph did wasn't because of a poor decision he made. It was because of a habit. He wasn't being malicious. He needed to do some work in his heart to develop good character qualities. He needed a new pattern of thinking and acting when he faced particular challenges.

When a habit develops, it bypasses the decision-making center of the brain. It takes work sometimes to form better habits to replace unhelpful ones. Our solution was to bring the actions back into the decision-making center of the brain and choose a different response. In Ralph's case, I identified the arena where he experienced the problem, chose a cue that would prompt him to take new actions, and inspired him to practice a new approach. With a focus on teaching, significant change took place in his life.

In the illustration above about Ralph, what specific things were part of the plan to help Ralph change?

_____

_____

_____

_____

_____

_____

Some Kids Resist Change

Not all kids are like Ralph. Some kids don't want to change. In that case, firmness makes their current patterns of living more uncomfortable, vision provides hope for a better way, and teaching gives specific steps needed to move forward.

> Kids need guidance and concrete plans to manage their struggles.

It's one thing to tell your child to be more kind, do his chores without being reminded, or to be honest, but most children need more than that. They need to know how to relate to an obnoxious brother, clean up a messy room, and have courage to overcome the temptation to lie. This is where the word "training" has its most important application.

The conscience provides children with promptings, but knowing what to do with the prompt can be a challenge. Kids need guidance and concrete plans to manage their struggles. They need to know what to say to themselves and what to do differently next time they face similar issues. As you study your child's weakness, you'll be able to provide ideas, suggestions, and plans to help your child overcome the temptation.

It's fascinating to watch kids change when they have specific strategies for moving forward. The four-year-old who continually interrupts needs to know how to handle his desires when others are in conversation. Mom may teach him that he needs to put his hand on her arm while she's talking to a friend. She, in turn, will put her hand on his hand, acknowledging with a silent signal, as she continues the dialogue with her friend. After a few moments, she will stop and address her son. This technique provides a simple introductory approach for a child to learn sensitivity and an appropriate way to interrupt. The child responds well because he has a plan, not just correction that says, "Stop interrupting."

By combining teaching with other concepts taught in earlier chapters we can maximize results. Often the key to making the plan work is to transfer responsibility to the child. If you give a plan to a child, you're likely to experience resistance. If you help the child develop the plan, ownership increases the likelihood of success. It's true that some children don't want to develop a plan, but this isn't optional. A child who is mean to his brother needs a plan for addressing the temptation to be unkind. Firmness requires working on the plan before the child goes back to playing. Parents then have the child look at the plan after each offense to add to it or adjust it. The combination of firmness, visioning, and teaching empowers children to change by clarifying the target, communicating why change is important, and providing a plan to get there.[11]

A Unique Plan for Each Child

In order to develop the teaching part of your strategy, you'll need to, again, study your child a bit. Use the space below to jot down some thoughts as you try to analyze patterns. Just take one area that you'd like to see your child change in and journal here about it.

What is the general problem you'd like to see changed? (E.g. angry outbursts, leaving messes around the house or in a specific room, or not turning assignments

---

[11]You might want to read Chapter 4 in *Motivate Your Child: A Christian Parent's Guide to Raising Kids Who Do What They Need to Do Without Being Told* to learn more about transferring responsibility to your child, a foundational concept in a heart-based approach.

in at school) And, in what arena would you like to work on this problem? (E.g. during homework, with siblings, during chores, etc.)

_____

_____

_____

_____

What are some solutions that you, as a parent, use in your own life to handle a similar situation? (E.g. ways you keep your anger under control, how you keep things neat, or how you turn things in on time)

_____

_____

_____

_____

What are some possible triggers for the child that could be part of the solution? (E.g. overwhelming feeling of emotion to implement a plan for anger, walking through a doorway to look back and evaluate messiness, or walking into class and asking, "What do I need to turn in?")

_____

_____

_____

_____

_____

It's important that you aren't quick to share the above ideas with your child. Rather, in order to transfer responsibility for the plan itself, you'll want to encourage your child to come to some of these ideas, or even better ones. Don't criticize a child's ideas, even if your experience tells you it won't work. Part of developing a strategy is trying new things. Sometimes kids have unrealistic ideas at first because of their limited life experience. That's okay. It's all part of the learning experience.

One boy told us that his plan for managing his anger was to lie flat in order to reduce his energy. We said, "Great. We'll be eager to hear how it goes for you."

The next week, when we asked him about his progress, he said, "That didn't work." But he found something else that did. He discovered that getting a drink of water when he was upset often helped him to calm down. So that became part of his plan.

Paying Attention to Inner Promptings

Part of the teaching process is helping your child understand more about the heart and the prompters that come from it. The conscience and the Holy Spirit provide internal prompters to do what's right. Recently, we were working with a six-year-old boy who was quite disrespectful to his mom, often saying "shut up" and other unkind things to her. He definitely needed a plan. He was a strong-willed little guy, and, as is often true, the behavior modification approaches used by Mom and others weren't working.

In one session, I (Scott) determined to teach him a bit more about the heart and how it prompts us to do the right thing. I asked him to stand in front of me, and I said, "Do you know where your heart is?"

> The conscience and the Holy Spirit provide internal prompters to do what's right.

"Yes, it's here," he said as he pointed to his chest.

"You're right. And did you know that it talks to you?"

"Yep."

I was impressed. This six-year-old already knew about the heart. So I continued the dialogue, "What does it say?"

He paused for a moment and said, "If I'm very quiet, then I can hear it say, 'babump, babump.'"

We all laughed and had fun in the next few minutes as I helped him understand that the physical heart beats, but the spiritual heart is where the emotions are and the patterns that we have are kept. It's also where God lives when we invite him in, and it's the place where the conscience prompts us. I whispered and said, "The heart will give you a reminder, 'Do the right thing.' Your job is to pay attention and do what's right."

Children at any age benefit from learning about the heart and its role in changing bad habits to good ones. You don't have to use words like sin, repentance, and forgiveness; your plan will embody these very concepts in practice. As you develop a plan for the specific challenge your child is facing, you'll be equipping that child with solutions that will be used even into adulthood.

Doreen and Charles knew they had a problem with Charlie. He lied often. He would lie to get out of trouble, to get something he wanted, and when retelling a story of something that happened, even when there seemed to be no benefit to the fabrication. They developed a plan to help their son build integrity.

Their plan involved firmness by stopping him when he started to spin a story instead of arguing with him about the facts. It seemed that the arguing tended to generate more lies. So, they simply said, "Stop talking. Either be quiet or start over." They used visioning to point out the benefits of integrity, such as trustworthiness, the privilege of privacy, and a clear conscience. They spent quite a bit of time on the teaching component, to help their son recognize what pressure was prompting the lie, how internal character could offset the temptation, and alternatives to lying.

One of the things they did in the teaching component was to talk about how honesty always occurs under pressure. It takes a person with strength on the inside to bear up under that pressure. They created an award and put it on the wall, looking for times that truth won because their son was able to be strong on the inside even when tempted to lie. During those times, they gave the award to him for a certain amount of time. Then, it returned to the wall until another honesty-over-lying time came around.

Dishonesty is a very difficult problem to address in any child. The most effective strategies for change use heart work

95

instead of behavior modification. Doreen and Charles saw signs of improvement in Charlie, but it took a lot of work, much dialogue, and regular doses of prayer for both wisdom in their approach and change in their son.[12]

Consider these things when you work on the teaching component with your child. How does your child learn best? How much can you accomplish in one setting? How are you doing in your relationship together? Are you experiencing closeness? Some parents overdo the lecture approach or try to teach during correction times. Those approaches are often weaker than the ones that consider the child's needs.

When was a time that you were successful in teaching your child in the past?

_____

_____

_____

_____

_____

_____

_____

---

[12] You might want to read Chapter 6 in the book *Motivate Your Child: A Christian Parent's Guide to Raising Kids Who Do What They Need to Do Without Being Told* to learn more about integrity and how to help kids be honest under pressure.

What are some approaches that work best with your child?

_____

_____

_____

_____

Teaching is an essential component of a good strategy. Spend some time studying your child and prepare helpful information about your child's issue.

Have a Meeting with Your Child

A child with a problem often resists correction. That's sometimes because of guilt or simply the fact that it's hard for anyone to address weaknesses openly. The meeting you have can be freeing if you focus on the solution, not just the problem. Teaching provides plans, and those plans often provide hope for the heart.

Take a few minutes and think about what your child can do in the challenging arena he's working on. What do you want instead, and how will your child accomplish this? What right thing can your child do to replace the unwanted behavior? Now plan how to present this teaching to your child.

> Teaching is an essential component of a good strategy.

Jamie, age seven, often fights with her brother. Mom is frustrated with continual bickering, put-downs, and rough words she hears exchanged between her kids. She is determined to do something about it. So, she plans her words carefully and chooses a time to talk to Jamie when she's alone. Here's what she said and why it worked. We've communicated the actual words

in quotes and the reasons for those words in parentheses.

Let me give you some ideas about how to work with your brother." (This conveys a desire to help, often opening the heart of a child to listen to advice.) "I know he can be annoying at times." (By communicating empathy like this, you further open the child's heart to your input.) "I see that you get frustrated with him and end up yelling or hitting him." (You have now clearly transferred responsibility to the child for her part of the problem.) "I've got some ideas that will make your life easier." (This speaks of hope and vision.) "I'd like to give you three choices to use when you start to get frustrated with your brother." (A thought-out plan that's made simple for a child further provides hope.) "You can ignore, confront, or get help." (This is a practical, doable approach for Jamie.)

Mom further shared how it's important to ignore without getting angry, confront without yelling, and get help without tattling. Jamie will need ongoing teaching and training, but now the struggles with her brother become the arena where learning takes place, new habits are developed, and progress is measured.

Mom will be successful with her daughter because she's helping her understand how to make progress, not just telling her to stop the unwanted behavior. Teaching shows kids how.

How did your meeting go? What did you learn? What worked?

_____

_____

_____

_____

_____

_____

_____

_____

_____

8

Spiritual Energy Provides Strength

We make adjustments; God creates total transformation.

Brian tells this story. "At thirteen years old, I had extreme anxiety that controlled me and my family. My parents are Christians and tried to help me, but I was stuck. We couldn't go out in public, and I often had panic attacks about things I feared. I would go around and check every window of the house and all the doors to make sure they were locked, not just at night, but several times during the day. Then, I met a counselor who helped me immensely. He told me about the power of the Holy Spirit and that one of the parts of the fruit of the Holy Spirit is peace.

"As he explained it to me, I knew I wanted the peace he was describing. I had never viewed the Holy Spirit as active in my heart, but I began to understand that my emotions were controlling me and that God had a solution for the problem in my life. I practiced yielding myself to the Holy Spirit through prayer, and I made a decision to let my fears go. It took quite a bit of work, but I realized I had spiritual resources. I had never experienced my Christian life like that before. In just a few short weeks, my anxiety was gone. I believe God did a miracle in my life that summer, and I now know more about the power of God in my life. I am free."

There's nothing like good theology about the heart to help parents recognize how limited human resources are. God is able to change the heart of a child. Some of the patterns children develop become quite ingrained. It takes much of God's grace working through thoughtful parents to see significant change in their children. If the goal is to move from point A to point B, then spiritual strength can make a huge difference. For example, prayer is an excellent tool to keep parents focused. Praying with your child is often quite effective, as well. God gives strength to address the weaknesses in our lives and those of our children. Praying parents are more sensitive to spiritual things happening in a child's heart. The Holy Spirit often works through the conscience, so tying spiritual resources to the conscience is a huge asset for anyone.

So far, we've talked about three of the components of a plan to move a child forward: firmness, visioning, and teaching. The fourth component will provide supernatural energy to empower change. We call this component "prayer," but this component encompasses spirituality in general to make the seemingly impossible possible.

The Power of the Holy Spirit

When it comes to internal motivation, there's nothing stronger than the power of the Holy Spirit to enact change. When anyone connects with this power, a supernatural element begins to work in the heart. Prayer is one of the vehicles God uses for us to connect with him, and yielding to the Holy Spirit is strategic.[13]

> The fourth component will provide supernatural energy to empower change.

Before we can take advantage of this important element, let's step back and address some key theological issues.

One dad said, "My son hasn't made a commitment to Christ. How can we use the work of the Holy Spirit in a child's life if he hasn't accepted Christ personally?"

That's a great question. It's true that, when people accept Jesus Christ, then the Holy Spirit takes up residence inside their hearts. We'll talk about how to connect children with the Holy Spirit in a bit, but first, what about the person who isn't yet a believer? What is the role of the Holy Spirit in that person's life?

We know from John 16:8 that the Holy Spirit convicts people who aren't Christians and the primary goal is to help them come to Christ. So, it's all the

---

[13] You might want to read Chapter 18 in the book *Motivate Your Child: A Christian Parent's Guide to Raising Kids Who Do What They Need to Do Without Being Told* to learn more about how to connect your child to the Holy Spirit and the power available to change even common areas of a person's life.

more important to help kids know that becoming a Christian is practical right now. It opens the door for the Holy Spirit to take up residence and begin to empower them to do what's right.

With a child who isn't yet a believer, you'll want to talk about the power of the Holy Spirit for those who trust Christ. Talk about it regularly. Young children sometimes grow into their faith in Christ, especially those who grow up in a Christian family. While teaching kids the importance of making a decision for Christ, we also practice spiritual disciplines such as praying out loud, reading God's Word, and attending worship services, even before children make a clear decision for Christ. So, you might add to that list of things we do in family life, the importance of being sensitive to the Holy Spirit's promptings. It's often those spiritual exercises and experiences that God uses to prompt a person, even a child, to make a profession of faith in Jesus Christ.

Furthermore, the Holy Spirit works in the heart of a nonbeliever. It's sometimes the inner prompting of God in a child's life that motivates greater awareness of right, wrong, and caring about others. It's those promptings that are often the early seeds of God's leading in a person's heart. You can talk about God's leadership even before that child is a believer and illustrate the sensitivity that comes from relying on him. As children grow into this awareness, salvation becomes closer than ever. God is at work in every person's life, and he regularly finds ways to connect with the human heart.[14]

> God is at work in every person's life, and he regularly finds ways to connect with the human heart.

If your child has made a commitment to Christ, then you'll want to talk about some of the practical benefits of that decision. A decision for Christ is not the end; it's only the beginning of an amazing walk of faith. The Holy Spirit takes up residence inside and actively works when we allow him to do so. We often ask a child who comes in for counseling, "Are you a Christian?" That

---

[14] You might want to read Chapter 17 in the book *Motivate Your Child: A Christian Parent's Guide to Raising Kids Who Do What They Need to Do Without Being Told* to learn how to lead your child to a personal decision to accept Christ.

question is sometimes met with a positive answer and a look of wonder, as if to say, "Yes, but I'm not here to talk about God. I'm here because I have a problem with anger." It's as if kids have a disconnect between their spiritual lives and their everyday experiences.

How Do You Experience the Power of God?

Brian's story about overcoming his anxiety with the help of the Holy Spirit is encouraging because it demonstrates what happens when a child gets connected to God's power in a personal way. Let's stop right here and ask a question about your own life. Have you ever experienced the power of God? Maybe God has changed someone you thought might never change, or maybe he worked out a situation that seemed impossible. Write something down here that God has done in your life that revealed his power.

_____

_____

_____

_____

_____

_____

This exercise is about you, and not your child, because it's important for you to know how to connect with God's power as you're teaching your child to do the same.

Take a moment and read the following scriptures and answer the questions.

What is one of the purposes of God's power as stated in 2 Corinthians 12:9? "But he said to me, 'My grace is sufficient for you, for my power is made perfect in weakness.'"

_____

_____

_____

_____

_____

What words are associated with the power of God in 2 Timothy 1:7? "For the Spirit God gave us does not make us timid, but gives us power, love and self-discipline."

_____

_____

_____

_____

_____

Read Philippians 2:13 "for it is God who works in you to will and to act in order to fulfill his good purpose." Sometimes we think we're alone in changing ourselves or our kids. How is this verse helpful in understanding the bigger picture of change in a person?

_____

_____

_____

_____

_____

The challenge is to engage this power in the heart of your child. Three tools can help you do this.

Three Spiritual Tools for Parents

1. Pray for your child.

Even if your child is unable or unwilling to pray, your prayers are significant. God often works through intercessors to accomplish his will. Your obedience to continually pray for your child is not only an acknowledgement that God is powerful but also a commitment to trust him. Pray that God will open significant conversations and bring experiences into your child's life that will contribute to new awareness and positive growth.

> The challenge is to engage this power in the heart of your child.

God has a plan for your child, and he wants to use you to be his hands and feet to reveal that plan. Praying for your child helps to ready your own heart for action. An amazing thing happens when we pray. Not only does God work in the life of the person we're praying for, but God also works in the life of the person praying. As you pray for your child, the Holy Spirit will make you more sensitive to what God is doing in your child's heart. You'll become more aware of teachable moments and more insightful with the words you share.

One day, a man came to Jesus begging for help for his son. In John 4:49, you can feel the urgency in his voice, "Sir, come down before my child dies." Jesus healed the boy, not because of the boy's faith, but because of a loving father who was willing to intercede and get help from the Lord for his son. As you come before God, you're asking him to use your faith and your commitment to be the vehicle he uses to provide the change.[15]

> God has a plan for your child, and he wants to use you to be his hands and feet to reveal that plan.

Take a moment and list three strengths you'd like to see developed more in your child and one weakness that needs some attention. Then share those things with God and ask him for ideas, wisdom, and opportunity for you to encourage your child.

Strengths

_____

_____

_____

Weakness

_____

---

[15] You might want to read Chapter 16 in the book *Motivate Your Child: A Christian Parent's Guide to Raising Kids Who Do What They Need to Do Without Being Told* to understand more about the spiritual warfare that takes place when you try to lead your home spiritually.

2. Pray with your child.

As you pray with your child, important lessons come to life about faith and how to come to God for personal issues. If your child is responsive to God, then the prayer offered by your child, when you pray together, should be strategic on your part. The prayer may ask God to remove the problem completely, but more importantly, the prayer should be that God would provide strength for the child to deal with that problem. God calls that strength "grace."

Julianne, age eight, came to her mom discouraged because God never answered her prayers. "I pray that God will help me with my anger, but he  doesn't take it away." This young girl was discouraged and disillusioned with God. Many children become disheartened because they don't get what they want when they ask God for things. Although asking God for specific things is okay, it's an advanced kind of prayer. The first type of prayer that children need to learn is to ask God to show them how they can fit into his plan.

We liked what Mom shared with her daughter. "Julianne, it sounds like your prayers have the wrong focus. If you want to watch God work in your life, then sometimes you might ask for God to reveal his power by changing things that you want changed, but more importantly, you want to come to God like this, 'Lord, what do you want me to do today for you?'"

Mom offered to share a verse with her daughter. "Julianne, there's a verse in the Bible just for you that I'd like to point out. Can I do that?"

Julianne was intrigued.

Mom opened the Bible to 1 Corinthians 10:13 and shared it this way. "Let me read it to you and explain each part."

"'No temptation has overtaken you' Your temptation to react to your anger is real. The feeling of anger isn't always wrong, but you're tempted to react to certain challenges with that anger, and that's when people get hurt and relationships get damaged.

"'...except what is common to mankind.' The problem you're experiencing is a common one. Other people have conquered this problem, and, as you overcome it yourself, you'll be able to help other people who are also tempted in this area.

"'And God is faithful;' You just need to know, Julianne, that God is reliable. He is in control. God's goal isn't just to make you happy. His goal is to grow you. But he doesn't want you to be overwhelmed either.

"'...he will not let you be tempted beyond what you can bear.' That's why this part of the verse is so important. God protects you and wants you to move forward in your life. He loves you and cares for you. He doesn't cause your temptations or create bad situations in your life, but when they come about, he protects you in them.

"'...But when you are tempted, he will also provide a way out' There's always another way to handle the situation. It will take practice to learn the ways of God. Those ways are sometimes different than you're currently using. But don't miss the last part of the verse, because sometimes people think that God is going to remove the situation, but for some reason he doesn't. Notice what it says.

God's goal isn't just to make you happy.

"'...so that you can endure it.' Many times, the solutions aren't to get out of the situation but to learn how to live rightly in them. That's important to understand."

The problem was that Julianne was focusing on her desires and wanting God to fit into her plans. Sometimes God graciously does that. But it's more valuable when a child seeks to fit into God's plans and asks God to reveal ways to do that. Then, children move toward a more others-centered way of living and a more God-directed life. It's in those moments that significant change takes place in the heart of a child, and that child has the privilege of watching God work.

As Julianne began to pray and ask God for direction, Mom also took her to God's Word where they looked up verses that related to the issues she was

working on. God began speaking to Julianne in some personal ways. Or, maybe it's better to say, that God was always willing to speak to Julianne, but Mom helped her learn how to listen.

Mom was thrilled when Julianne took it upon herself to encourage her grandpa. They had talked about how he was feeling a bit discouraged. When he came over, Julianne went up to him and gave him a big hug and said, "Grandpa, I love you." It was touching, and, that evening, Mom asked Julianne what prompted her to do such a kind thing. She said, "I just felt a prompting on the inside to cheer him up. I knew it's what God wanted me to do." It was fun for Mom to see Julianne connecting with God's inner promptings in her life.[16]

If your child is willing to pray for strength, then take advantage of that desire. However, sometimes kids aren't ready to pray or don't know how to pray in those moments. You can still pray with your child and model relying on God and asking him for strength. Sometimes, children need to rely on the faith of a praying parent for a while, until they learn how to come to God for themselves.

3. Engage your child with God's power.

In the same way that children go through physical developmental stages, they also go through stages of spiritual development. Some of this has to do with their ability to comprehend certain truths, and another part of it has to do

---

[16] You might want to read Chapter 14 in the book *Motivate Your Child: A Christian Parent's Guide to Raising Kids Who Do What They Need to Do Without Being Told* to learn more fun and practical ways to connect kids to the Bible. You'll learn how Jesus used creativity and life experience and how you can energize your own Bible time with your kids.

with responsiveness to God and his leadership. For example, young children can find trust rather easy since it's a regular part of their lives. Teenagers, however, often question their faith. That's not a bad thing. It just means that they need good answers to those questions in order to fully solidify their faith and make it a personal one. A wise parent will be open about spirituality and talk about God in appropriate ways, given the development stage of the child.

> When children learn how to rely on God's grace, then amazing things happen.

Here's where some important theology helps kids gain a new understanding of change in their own lives. Sometimes, children have a view of God that he is some kind of policeman, monitoring their activities and ready to arrest them if they do the wrong thing. This often happens when kids get an understanding that God is omniscient—that he knows all—and that he is holy and just. Those are important theological ideas to understand for anyone. However, only focusing on those qualities gives kids an imbalanced view of God.

Another aspect of God's work in our lives has to do with grace. Grace has several facets, but one of them is that it's divine energy to manage the challenges of life right now. God gives grace to people to help them manage their anger, relate effectively to a parent when asked to do something hard, and to hang in there with difficult homework. When children learn how to rely on God's grace, then amazing things happen.

Many times kids are willing to receive from God. They just need to know how to obtain his grace and apply it to their situation. Fourteen-year-old Katie was often upset when injustice took place, especially when it happened to her. She was sometimes mistreated by friends, by her coach, and even by her dad. These mistreatments all seemed to be genuine as she shared the stories of what actually happened. The problem wasn't just external, though. A problem was also growing in Katie's heart. She was developing bitterness inside, and it was increasing her anger level.

Dad shared with her the passage in 1 Peter 2:18-23 that talked about suffering unjustly. The verse that helped her the most was verse 23, which spoke about Christ as our example of unjust suffering. It says, "He entrusted himself to him who judges justly." Dad described it as putting the justice of the world into a suitcase and giving it to God to manage. Katie began placing her trust in God, and the spiritual solution for the injustices of her personal life produced significant results.

Not all children are responsive, spiritually. When they are, there are many biblical truths that can change the way they think and act. Kids who are resistant to God and to his Word, however, often need some extra spiritual influence in their lives. Requiring church activities, finding spiritual mentors, and sharing your personal spiritual insights can go a long way to mold a child's thinking.

As you share God with your child, be sure to have a balanced approach. Sometimes parents use the scriptures to tell kids what they can't do or to show how God hates sin or isn't pleased with certain activities. The holiness, justice, and wrath of God are true and right. But Jesus was careful to help his disciples see the value of viewing God as a father who is loving, compassionate, and caring about the intricate needs of a person. Jesus told his disciples in Matthew 6:26 that the Father takes care of them just like he takes care of the birds. Jesus continued to develop their thinking in Matthew 10:30 by telling them that the Father has every hair of their head numbered. When kids catch a glimpse of the personal care of God, then they learn to trust him and yield themselves to God in specific ways.[17]

What are some of the spiritual influences in your child's life? And what are some others that you might seek to cultivate?

_____

_____

_____

[17] You might want to read Chapter 15 in the book *Motivate Your Child: A Christian Parent's Guide to Raising Kids Who Do What They Need to Do Without Being Told* to learn ways to help kids practice their faith.

What are some things about God and his Word that you would like for your child to believe in order to help your child right now in life?

_____

_____

_____

Spiritual Warfare is Real

Satan hinders progress in a family in a variety of ways. Ephesians 4:26-27 says, "In your anger do not sin: Do not let the sun go down while you are still angry, and do not give the devil a foothold." Emotional intensity is often a way that Satan hinders spiritual vitality. But that's only one of Satan's schemes. He loves to derail progress, kill spiritual growth, and hinder closeness in a family. The best way to fight Satan's attack is to use the spiritual resources provided by God himself, including prayer and the truth of his Word.

Don't let discouragement hinder your forward progress. Expect resistance and be prepared for it. Your attitude can make all the difference. When you base your motivation on your convictions instead of on results, you're able to do what needs to be done even when things get hard.

It's exciting to watch children grow spiritually. Look for ways to reveal that the Bible is relevant to their lives. Provide opportunities to see God work by serving, attending church, and sharing your personal stories of answered prayers. Any problem a child is experiencing can be helped through spiritual resources. Spend some time thinking and working in this area, and it will enhance your plan greatly.

> Satan hinders progress in a family in a variety of ways.

 ## Have a Meeting with Your Child

Children are at different places in their spiritual receptivity. The child's openness to the Lord will determine how this meeting goes. For a child who is resistant to the Lord, be sure to emphasize the grace and mercy of God and the benefits of the Christian life. One dad, working with his seventeen-year-old son, often told stories about people at work and elsewhere that got themselves into trouble. Why? It was because they were continually trying to live a life that was the opposite of God's way. God designed the world and set up the principles that make it work. Not just gravity, but also things that have to do with integrity and relationships.

If your child is in the exploring stage, then you'll want to point out intriguing things about life and how God works. Have fun devotions and talk about how practical God's Word is for our lives. Shirley told us how she and her daughters looked for God-moments in the course of the day. Her children were on the lookout for spiritual activity. Great conversations came out of those sharing times.

If your child is spiritually sensitive and committed to Christ, look for opportunities to share spiritually what God is teaching you and ask questions about what God is teaching your child. You can learn from your son or daughter, who is a brother or sister in Christ. You might say, "What is God teaching you? I'd like to learn more."

Whatever the level of spiritual sensitivity in your children, you want to try to increase spiritual dialogue with them. Faith is an important part of who you are, and it should come out in how you talk and how you interact in life. Influencing others spiritually takes place naturally when you're living your life for Christ. It's not forced.

God is in the business of changing people, so regular talks about him and his work should be part of your plan to move your child from point A to point B.

How did your meeting go? What did you learn? What worked?

_____

_____

_____

_____

_____

_____

_____

_____

9

Coaching Sets the Attitude

Most kids want happiness, unless it involves change.

Tim realized that he needed to make a change in the way he worked with his nine-year-old son, Paul. Tim loved his son a lot and wanted the best for him, but he realized that he was becoming harsh and intense in his approach. Distance was replacing the close relationship he desired.

The adjustments Tim made were strategic and not only strengthened the relationship between father and son, but they also helped Paul do better in one particular area of his life. The big change Tim made was to move from a policeman attitude with his son to a coaching attitude. The change in Tim was prompted by playing on the church softball team. The coach had a way of working with the players that encouraged them to do well. Sometimes players would get discouraged, and the coach demonstrated several good strategies that spurred people on.

Tim talked to the coach about his philosophy of coaching, and the coach referred to a scripture that opened new ideas for Tim. Galatians 6:9 says, "Let us not become weary in doing good, for at the proper time we will reap a harvest if we do not give up."

"Coaching is about helping people not give up. When players get discouraged or tired, then they go back to bad habits. My job is to help them move forward."

The coach also referred to Hebrews 10:24. "'And let us consider how we may spur one another on toward love and good deeds.' As a coach, that's also my job. I don't want to simply tell players what they're doing wrong. I'd rather encourage them to continue figuring out how to do the right thing."

He was driven by the belief that "wrong actions require a consequence."

Tim started to think about how he could coach his son. He believed that changing his approach would make him more effective as a dad. This was major for Tim because he had to deal with some of his underlying beliefs about his job as a parent. He started to adjust the way he related to the members of his family. He even let his son give him some advice about those changes, something quite different than he ever would have done before.

One of the most important areas of change for Tim took place in correction.

It used to be that he would focus more on what his son did wrong and tie it to a consequence. He was driven by the belief that "wrong actions require a consequence." Now, instead of simply giving consequences for offenses and emphasizing justice, Tim started studying his son, finding out what was going on inside of him, and offering him solutions to overcome the roadblocks that were getting in the way. The other key components of an action plan for change—firmness, visioning, teaching, and prayer—were important, but a coaching attitude made all the difference. Now he was approaching his son's mistakes by encouraging him along to overcome them. Tim moved from punishment to training.

Coaching is another key component of an action plan for change. As you'll recall, firmness makes point A uncomfortable and motivates change. Visioning answers the question "Why?" and offers hope for future benefits. Teaching tells the child "How?" and helps the child to develop a plan for success. Prayer is essential for working where God is working and empowering heart change. Coaching keeps the parent and child on the same team and offers strength to the relationship.[18]

Dad Became Part of the Solution Instead of Contributing to the Problem

One major temptation for Paul was to be mean to his mom, often mistreating her when he didn't like what she asked him to do or when she reacted in anger to him. Tim's usual response to his son was to back up his wife by becoming angry and defensive, resulting in distance and further tension in all of their relationships.

As Tim considered this idea of coaching his son toward change, he decided to take a completely different approach. He met with his wife first and told her what he was going to do. "I'm going to try to teach Paul a different way to relate to you. It will likely still involve firmness, but I'm going to help him understand

---

[18] You might want to read Chapter 5 in the book *Motivate Your Child: A Christian Parent's Guide to Raising Kids Who Do What They Need to Do Without Being Told* to learn how to help kids think rightly about their offenses and mistakes instead of blaming, rationalizing, or justifying themselves.

you better and develop some skills to relate to you more effectively. I know that sometimes you get frustrated with him, and I want him to understand how to respond to you in more effective ways. His current response is wrong and it isn't working. Any ideas you have would be helpful."

As Tim listened to his wife, he learned that her angry responses often came when she either felt desperate that Paul wasn't responding or hurt and violated by his cutting remarks. Tim used those ideas to develop a new coaching plan. He knew that he might give his wife some suggestions about how she could approach the conflict better, but first, he needed to figure out some solutions for Paul. As the ideas began to come, he sometimes ran them by his wife, and she seemed responsive to the suggestions. She seemed to feel a greater sense of support and, remarkably, her attitude began to change as well as she worked with Paul.

In Tim's meeting with Paul, he started with these words to set the stage with some affirmation and a positive approach. "Paul, I want to help you with some strategies for working with Mom. I think there are things that you can do to decrease the tension and increase the close relationships we all want to have in our home. I thought I could give you some ideas that might help you be more successful. I think you get stuck sometimes, and then you become mean, and that heads things down a bad path. I'd like to help you.

"It seems like you need ideas in a couple of areas. One is when Mom asks you to do something you'd rather not do. Other times, it's just the timing of her request or the way she approaches you. In each situation, you get frustrated and then react in unhelpful ways. Sometimes Mom makes mistakes in the way she relates to you, but she really does want your best and wants to have a close relationship with you.

"I can give you some strategies for each of those challenges so that you can respond better. And, here's the hidden benefit. If you can learn how to relate better to us, then God will use those skills in your life in the future. You'll be more successful at relating to others as well. You'll always find situations where you're asked to do something you don't want to do. Now's a great time to practice responding well, but it means learning some new things about how to respond under pressure."

Tim tried to use a conscience-based approach to reach his son's heart. He talked about compassion and the importance of caring about others and how they feel. If he could help his son think about the situation from a broader perspective and see that they were all imperfect people, and that Mom had feelings too, then Paul might respond better.[19]

"I'd like to coach you along in this," Tim continued. "If you act out and are mean to your mom, I may have to discipline you, but more importantly, I want to help you develop new ideas of how to move forward in a positive way. If you find yourself stuck, come see me, and we'll talk about it."

Paul was responsive to his dad's approach. Tim encouraged Paul to look for ways he could help our around the house. When Tim saw his son take initiative to set the table, he winked at him in affirmation. Paul shared some of his concerns about Mom, and Dad empathized with the challenge that his son experienced. Then, they looked for ways to help Paul change his response and do what's right.

> Tim tried to use a conscience-based approach to reach his son's heart.

Change took some time. Dad often felt himself sliding back into his old policeman stance, but he would stop and readjust. There were times that Tim didn't know what to do, and he just had to be quiet while he tried to figure something out instead of getting sucked into the interaction. He sometimes would say to his wife, "I've got an idea for you about how to relate to Paul in a way that might be more effective." He said something similar to his son. Over time, Paul tried some of his dad's suggestions

---

19 You might want to read Chapter 7 in the book *Motivate Your Child: A Christian Parent's Guide to Raising Kids Who Do What They Need to Do Without Being Told* to learn more about helping children develop compassion and care about others.

and others of his own. He was not so quick to speak. He appealed to his mom more graciously and, many times, did what she asked even when her delivery wasn't the best.

Changes Often Need to Take Place in Parents First

Tim was an agent for healing in his family because he chose to make a change in himself. Tim first had to adjust his approach. That new way of working with both his wife and his son paid off with some significant benefits. You can do in your family what Tim did in his. You can be the change agent in your home and start the ball rolling to reduce tension, increase closeness, and help others respond in better ways. Learning how to be a coach to your child is a great place to begin. Here are some tips.

1. It's not good enough to be right; you also need to be wise.

Sometimes parents see something wrong, know the right thing that should be done, but give little attention to how they present it. A good coach not only considers the challenges of the situation, but also seeks to find a way to present the solutions well.

For Mary Beth, the issue was timing. She realized that pulling back a bit and planning her response to the sibling conflict in her home was often more productive. Sometimes, on the spot, she would have to separate her kids and have them each take a break to calm down. That slowed the process, bought her a little time to compose herself, and often prevented a further escalation of tension in the home. When emotions settled a bit, Mary Beth's correction was often accepted with less resistance.

> Tim was an agent for healing in his family because he chose to make a change in himself.

For Frank, the solution was in his tone of voice. He realized that when he was correcting his kids, his tone escalated. When he intentionally reduced the intensity of his tone with his teenage daughters, he was surprised by their willingness to listen to him. His softer approach communicated teamwork and had a significant impact on the family dynamic.

Confrontation can be more successful when you combine what you know to be right with a wise approach. Don't confuse thoughtfulness with a lack of firmness. Good coaches know how to apply both. Consider these two verses and answer the question, "What suggestions does the Bible give when facing a challenging situation?"

Galatians 6:1 says, "Brothers and sisters, if someone is caught in a sin, you who live by the Spirit should restore that person gently. But watch yourselves, or you also may be tempted."

Proverbs 15:1 states, " A gentle answer turns away wrath, but a harsh word stirs up anger."

How do you think you might be wiser in approaching the challenges with your child?

_____

_____

_____

_____

2. Focus on the goal, not on the problem.

Although a discussion of the problem may be appropriate, it's focusing on

the goal that makes the coach most successful with his players. Sometimes parents can get stuck focusing on what the child shouldn't do or what the child is doing wrong. A coaching attitude helps the child focus forward, looking ahead to a better response.

We've already talked in previous chapters about communicating vision and identifying the character quality that the child needs to develop. The key in this chapter is to bring those changes into your attitude. An attitude is a mindset toward a particular trigger. Attitudes come automatically in our lives and, if we're not careful, can take us in a negative direction. You might have a positive attitude toward Starbucks or solving math problems but a negative attitude

> A coaching attitude helps the child focus forward, looking ahead to a better response.

toward fast food or shoveling snow. The challenge comes when those attitudes start affecting your responses without realizing it. Off-handed comments toward negative things, or defensiveness about things you value, can get in the way of effective communication.

A positive approach with your child can propel effective change. You will still need the other components of firmness, visioning, teaching, and prayer. Kids are imperfect people and often need a lot of work to move forward, but thinking and focusing on the goal can make all the difference.

Which of the components come easier to you? Might you be more attracted to vision and relationship? Or firmness and teaching? Evaluate your own strengths and tendencies and jot them down here.

_____

_____

_____

_____

_____

3. Tailor your coaching style to the needs of your players.

There's not just one way to coach. Each coach develops his or her own style. In the same way, each parent has unique gifts, strengths, and personalities. Those couples that overemphasize uniformity in parenting can miss the benefits of each parent's uniqueness. For example, Dads always do it differently than moms. Always. If you allow the differences to create frustration between you, marital harmony will decrease. Rather, value the strengths you see in your mate.

Sometimes those strengths are complicated by weaknesses, but value the strength and provide suggestions to overcome the weaknesses.

The same is true with your child. Sometimes parents assume that their strengths are the best approach for the child. For example, a parent who is strong in relationships may chose to use warmth, kindness, and gentleness to try to move a child forward. That's not bad, but the question is, "Is that approach what my child needs?" Just because you have strength in the area of connecting relationally, doesn't mean that your child thrives in a non-structured approach to parenting. Don't get us wrong. Relationship is always important, but some kids need more firmness than others, and those parents who use relationship as the tool to accomplish almost everything may find that their kids don't appreciate the seriousness of some of their responsibilities.

There are a lot of good ways to raise kids.

On the other hand, sometimes a parent will overemphasize firmness when a child needs more relationship. Couples often find that one of them is more firm and the other is more relational in their approach. There are a lot of good ways to raise kids. There's not just one way, and not even one good, Christian way. God has made us each unique, and that uniqueness comes out in the way we work with our children.

You can raise godly, responsible kids using a relational approach, and you can raise godly, responsible kids using a firm approach. The question isn't so much about what approach is right. The question is, "What approach is right for my child at this particular time?" A good coach knows how to change the approach because the child needs something different to move forward. Many parents find it necessary to make personal changes that are outside of their comfort zones in order to reach a child's specific needs. That's good coaching and the sign of a wise parent.

Do you generally find your child more responsive to a firm approach or a relational approach? Can you think of an example?

4. Study your child.

Each child is unique and different. When developing parenting solutions, you don't want to fall into the one-size-fits-all trap. Sometimes parents develop a solution and apply it to all their kids. Other times parents get an idea from a neighbor or friend that worked in their family and simply try to use it. Ideas are great, and you may find them from a number of sources. But you must choose wisely how to apply them with your child.

As you study your child, look for areas of strength and find ways to take those strengths and apply them to a weakness. For example, AnnaMae saw that her son was emotionally sensitive, easily excitable, and a lot of fun to be around. Unfortunately, he also had a challenge with anger episodes. She affirmed his emotional sensitivity and even used it to help him develop self-control by showing him how his anger was hurting others. Because he could connect emotionally with others, that helped him with the internal motivation to make some changes.

Warren saw that his daughter was quite responsible, but she didn't seem to care about others who were hurt. Both of those are conscience issues, so he complimented her for her responsibility and challenged her to use that same internal obligation to help her take concern for others, not just herself.

Each child has unique triggers, tendencies, and challenges. If you can connect with that uniqueness, then a child is often more willing to see your help as a benefit instead of as a criticism. Furthermore, each child has to overcome internal thinking errors and poor habits of relating. Considering all of these unique differences can equip you with more strategic solutions.

What are some of your child's strengths? What are some triggers, or thinking challenges, your child experiences?

_____

_____

_____

_____

5. Think strategy instead of rules.

Rules tend to be confining. Although they are helpful to keep people on track, an overemphasis on rules can hinder a coaching attitude with a child. Parents who focus on rules tend to react. Those who focus on strategy tend to encourage. You don't have to get rid of the rules. In fact, every home has them and rules are needed to clarify expectations and keep things moving in a good way. The challenge is to keep rules in perspective as you direct and redirect your child.

Remember that you aren't teaching rules; you're teaching children. When a child violates a rule, firmness and correction are likely in order. However, in the midst of your correction, be sure to demonstrate value for the child as well. Your goal is to move a child on a map from point A to point B. An infraction of a rule is a setback but not a failure.

Pam wanted to react less and plan more as she worked with her daughter, Rachel. She realized that her tendency, when she saw something wrong, was to yell or bark some kind of command. It was often some kind of surprise that set her off, so she determined to react more slowly when something happened.

For example, Rachel came into the house with dirty shoes and was tracking dirt inside. Pam felt her heart jump and almost started yelling, but stopped herself mid-breath. She quickly said, "Rachel, whoa, stop for a minute." Rachel paused and looked up. "It looks like we have a problem. Look behind you." Rachel looked and realized what she had done. Mom said, "Take your shoes

off right there and carry them back outside, then you can help me clean up the mess." Pam was pleased that she handled the problem without the anger. She solved the problem and showed value to her daughter at the same time.

Another way to demonstrate a coaching attitude is to look for ways to affirm "approximately right" behavior to move your child forward on the path. Sometimes kids make changes that others don't notice or the changes are inconsistent. That's what happened to Christopher. He determined, at age eleven, to be less annoying and more helpful in his home. He actually thought he was doing pretty well after one week. In fact, his parents even saw it. But when we asked his siblings if they saw any change, they said, "Nothing is different." That was discouraging to Christopher. Dad and Mom encouraged their son to keep making forward progress, and it wasn't long before everyone noticed the difference.

Change takes time, and a negative reputation is a hard thing to overcome. Just continue doing what's right and seek to please God. Help kids see that their goal isn't to be people pleasers but God pleasers. Do what's right, even if others don't notice. Parents become coaches as they encourage the small steps of progress each day.

What are some ideas that come to your mind of ways you can encourage your child toward change?

_____

_____

_____

_____

A coaching attitude with your child is strategic and can catapult your child to significant change. It focuses on the goal, but more importantly, it helps you, as the parent, develop a more thoughtful and intentional approach to change. It puts you and your child on the same team and strengthens your relationship together. So, go out there and win the game, draw your team together, and take the necessary steps to move your child toward the goal.

Have a Meeting with Your Child

Coaching meetings are crucial. They communicate a positive sense of moving forward, but they don't ignore the problem. The question a good coach asks is, "How can I help you move from where you are to where you need to be?" Of course, some children don't want to change, and they'll need visioning and firmness to help them see the need. Putting it all together with a coaching attitude will win in the end.

Some kids seem bent on pushing the limits and doing the wrong thing. They seem to want to do their own research by wandering outside the boundaries. They need to see both from you and through life, that there's a way to live that is good. Bad things happen when we violate God's standard. Some kids want to learn that lesson through experience. It's your job as a parent to point out the consequences in life, point the way to the right path, and continually look for opportunities to reach the heart.

> Parents become coaches as they encourage the small steps of progress each day.

As you coach your child, seek to be encouraging. "Son, I noticed that you've been managing yourself better with your brother. I saw you trying to calm him down and get him to change. I like the way you were trying to be a peacemaker with him. I know that he doesn't always respond the right way, but I wanted to encourage you and tell you that I see that you're trying."

It's easier to move someone in the direction of a goal if you can notice and appreciate "approximately right" behavior and focus on the internal motivation that's prompting that initiative. Parents sometimes tend to have negative meetings with their kids that continually point out the problem. But noticing and highlighting positive steps of improvement, even if they're small, is extremely motivating.

How did your meeting go? What did you learn? What worked?

_____

_____

_____

_____

_____

_____

_____

_____

_____

10

Building Motivation from Within

Good character is simply the combination of good habits.

Once you have the tools in place as mentioned in the previous chapters, then you're ready to help kids move from point A, where they are now, to point B, where they need to be. You'll use firmness to make point A uncomfortable, visioning to attract them to point B, teaching to show them "how," prayer to provide strength, and coaching to create an attitude of support to move toward the goal. All of this will take place in the context of strong relationship.

In this chapter, you'll learn a specific technique that will help you use all of those things to build internal motivation so that the child isn't always relying on the parent to move forward.

We call it "The Three C's of Internal Motivation." They are cue, conscience, and character. These three things together help kids learn to take initiative and empower them to manage themselves better.[20]

Cue, Conscience, and Character

Eight-year-old Jack is another boy we worked with who was having a problem in school. He talks at times when it's not appropriate. The teacher's plan for correction is to tape a card to Jack's desk and, every time he talks out, she says, "Jack, give yourself another mark for talking." Jack then has to put a tally mark on the card and, at the end of the day, the card goes home with Jack for a parent's signature.

The teacher's plan is helpful in that it's calling attention to the problem so that Jack can see it more clearly. The weakness with this approach is that Jack is only learning about the problem and doesn't have a solution for it. He was disappointed in himself that he kept getting tally marks, but he wasn't changing. We helped him, his parents, and the school develop a different plan that moved away from behavior modification to more of a heart-based solution. It worked in just a few weeks, with immediate change taking place in a few days. Here's what we did.

---

[20] You might find it helpful to read Chapter 8 in **Motivate Your Child: A Christian Parent's Guide to Raising Kids Who Do What They Need to Do Without Being Told** to learn more about helping your child take initiative. When kids see what needs to be done and do it, then they start moving toward maturity.

1. Transfer Responsibility to the Child

We discussed the problem with Jack and had him explain the arena where he was tempted to talk when he should be quiet instead. We described the arena as the place where the action happens.

> By involving children in the process of developing the plan, we gain greater commitment to the solution.

Jack determined that his arena for talking inappropriately happened in two places. First, he was tempted to talk when he finished classwork before his classmates and had to wait for them. Second, he was tempted to talk when switching between subjects. He also identified a friend named Bill that he tended to talk with at the wrong times. Now we had the arenas, and we were ready to develop the plan.

Sometimes parents have good ideas about a particular plan that would solve the child's problem. You could go through this whole process on your own as a parent, and then just hand the plan to your child. In fact, that's how many parents do it. But just giving a child a plan, doesn't ensure motivation to implement it. By involving children in the process of developing the plan, we gain greater commitment to the solution.

What kinds of words can you use that transfer responsibility to your child? You might want to look at the interaction above for answers or choose your own ideas.

_____

_____

_____

_____

2. Identifying the Cue

"Jack, how do you know when you're in the arena? We need a cue or some kind of signal to remind you that it's time to implement your plan. It sounds like you finish your classwork before your classmates. Is that true?"

"Yes."

"We need some kind of a cue that you're done."

"I usually put my pencil down."

"That's perfect. We can use that as your cue."

Cues are present in every situation, and those who recognize them know when to act. Sometimes those cues are external, such as a calendar. You wake up and see that it's Tuesday and know that you need to take the trash down to the street. Other times the cues are internal. You feel that gut feeling of anger, and you know that you better implement your anger plan or you'll explode.

Parents, for example, rely on cues such as a clock or a to-do list to keep kids moving. Then, the parent becomes the cue for the child. The child waits until Dad gives an instruction that then becomes the cue to act. If we're going to develop internal motivation we want to connect the children directly with the cues. For example, Ted's job is to take the dog out. Mom is frustrated because she continually has to tell Ted to do it. What is Mom's cue that it's time to take the dog out? The dog whines at the door. In order for Mom to transfer responsibility to her son, she has to connect Ted with the cue. Now, instead of saying, "Ted, take out the dog," Mom says, "Ted, do you hear it?" Ted eventually learns to hear the dog whining instead of relying on Mom's cue to act. Connecting kids to cues teaches them to act independently.

> Cues are present in every situation, and those who recognize them know when to act.

What kind of cues might be the prompters in the following illustrations? They might already exist and you simply draw attention to them, or you may need to create a cue that will signal the appropriate action.

Dawdling in the morning _____

Disrespect when given a "no" answer _____

Forgetting to turn homework in _____

Leaving the bathroom a mess _____

Cue   Conscience   Character

Do it!

3. Cultivate the Conscience

Identifying the cue is sometimes all that a child needs to become more self-motivated. But most children also need the next step, which is to articulate their response. Again, the child helps to develop the plan.

To do this with Jack, we drew a T-chart on a piece of paper. At the very top, we wrote the title, "Jack's Plan for Talking at the Wrong Time." Over the left column, we wrote "Jack," and over the right column, we wrote the word "Ideas." Then we were ready to go to work.

"Jack, what are some things you could do or say to yourself in that moment when you put the pencil down that will help you to remember to not talk?"

"I could remind myself to be quiet."

"That's good. What exact words would you say to yourself?"

The reason we want Jack to identify the exact words is because those words will become the prompting of the conscience and will help Jack to be internally motivated to do the right thing. Psalm 19:14 says, "May these words of my mouth and this meditation of my heart be pleasing in your sight, Lord, my Rock and my Redeemer." In this case, it's the meditations of the heart that we're focusing on.

Through some dialogue, we chose the exact words that Jack could say to himself. We decided that he would say, "Wait quietly." In addition, Jack decided to add a few more things to his plan. He could double-check his work. He could look up at the teacher to remind him to do the right thing. And when he looked at his friend Bill, he would remind himself about the importance of sticking to his plan.

We encouraged the teacher to add to the existing card so that after she told Jack to add a tally mark, she would ask him, "What's your plan?" This would remind Jack to look at the card on his desk and read the words "Wait quietly."

As you're developing the plan using the T-chart with your child, be careful to let the child do the writing and to have him only write what will work for him. We explained to Mom that it's essential that she not write anything down under the Jack column. Remember, we are transferring responsibility to Jack. This is Jack's plan. Jack is the one who needs to write those things down. However, the right-hand side, under the word "Ideas," is the place where others can share their thoughts. Mom, Dad, teachers, and other students all may offer Jack suggestions for achieving his goal. Only the ideas that will work for Jack are the ones he'll transfer to the left-hand side of the T-chart.

Twelve-year-old Marcy was in continual conflict with her parents about leaving the bathroom a mess. Previous attempts at punishment weren't working. Marcy wasn't changing. Dad and Mom decided to use the three C's to see if that might help, and it did! Marcy decided to put a sign on the back of the door that said, "Oops!" The words that she would say to herself were, "Turn around and check," Those words would remind her to look and see if the floor was cleaned up and the things on the counter were straightened.

The conscience prompts kids to do what's right. With some training using scripted words, the conscience can provide specific guidance. However, the words used are important. Some children have negative words playing in their heads that focus on inadequacy, weakness, and failure. The words you want in this plan should propel kids forward, not point out their weaknesses.

What are some ways that you can train the conscience of your child so that it has more of a coaching prompting than a condemning tone?

_____

_____

_____

_____

4. Build Character

The conscience doesn't clean a bathroom, stop talking in class, or take a dog outside. That's why the third C, character, is so important. Jack needs to develop self-control to stop talking. Ted needs to develop awareness in order to hear the dog whining. Marcy needed to develop initiative to clean the bathroom. In all of these cases, parents discussed the character quality with the child and looked for ways to build it.

> With some training using scripted words, the conscience can provide specific guidance.

Remember that a character quality is a pattern of thinking and acting in response to a challenge. It takes time to learn new ways to think and act. Character is built over time. Using all of the tools in this action plan in a concerted way builds new patterns for handling particular challenges. Significant change takes place in the heart. And new patterns of relating or handling life replace the old patterns, as kids learn new ways of responding to the temptations they face.

Recently, a fourteen-year-old young man, Anthony, who had been part of our counseling program, came back to visit us with his mom, Sophia. The interesting thing about this situation is that Mom had been particularly discouraged when she came to us earlier because her husband wasn't willing to help or be part of the solution. In fact, he often made things worse with his anger and sarcasm, further damaging his relationship with their son.

It was great to hear the progress that their family had made. We asked the young man what kind of differences he saw in himself now. He said that he had learned to be nicer. But his mom smiled and filled in some of the gaps. "He has become more thoughtful of others and more self-controlled. Those are the two things we worked on, and that work paid off. He's much more enjoyable to be with, and he feels better about himself, as well. Yesterday, I came home with a load of groceries. Anthony was watching TV, but when he saw me, he jumped up to help me. That wouldn't have happened a couple of months ago. Things have really changed."

I asked them how Dad was working into their plan and progress. Sophia nodded. "He still gets angry at times, but he's coming around. He's seeing how I work with Anthony, and I see him trying some of those things, as well, because they're working."

Anthony chimed in. "I don't react to my dad's anger now, and it seems to improve the situation."

This family still has some work to do, but the progress is encouraging.[21]

Daniel was another one of our success stories. He was a ten-year-old pitcher on a Little League team, and he had a significant anger problem. Daniel identified that the cue that sparked his anger was a series of bad pitches. One bad pitch wasn't the problem. It's when he had several in a row. So we helped him identify some things he could say to himself while on the mound when his pitching wasn't going as well as he liked. Sometimes, he would just laugh it off. Other times, he would tell himself to focus on the next pitch. Still other times, he would critique what he did wrong, such as dropped his shoulder or started with his feet in the wrong place. As he developed a plan to listen to cues and activate his conscience, his anger diminished greatly, creating better character qualities.

> Motivation is usually prompted by the question, "Why?"

It wasn't long before Daniel was telling the rest of the players on the team that they needed to go see Dr. Turansky. We ended up conducting an anger workshop for the parents and the players. Parents and children alike found the solutions helpful, and the children noticed that they could use them on the playing field and elsewhere. Essentially, we helped them develop self-control by developing a personalized plan.

5. Why?

Motivation is usually prompted by the question, "Why?" Here's what a series of questions prompted by "Why?" could look like: "Why should I do this? What am I going to get out of it? Are you going to give me something? Are you going to pay me?" Those who are motivated internally ask different questions and seek different answers than those who are motivated externally. They want to feel a sense of accomplishment from mastering a skill, reaching a goal, or achieving an objective. They are prompted by a sense of purpose or progress in their lives

---

[21] You might consider reading Chapter 20 in the book *Motivate Your Child: A Christian Parent's Guide to Raising Kids Who Do What They Need to Do Without Being Told* for more ideas about trying to lead your family when the other parent isn't on board or if you're parenting on your own.

and the fact that they and others are seeing maturity and growth. They like to see how their contribution fits into the bigger picture.

Keep it simple and ask your child the question, "Why do you want to keep your room clean, talk less in class, or gain control of your anger?" The answer can be defined, written down, and repeated regularly. That motivation has to do with the heart and its desires. The conscience provides the continual reminder.

Just to practice this idea, take a moment and ask yourself why working on these behaviors is helpful for a child's life.

Keep room clean _____

Talk less in class _____

Gain control of anger _____

For Jack, who talked at inappropriate times in class, his answer to why he wanted to improve in this area was this: "I want to be known as a guy who is thoughtful about others." That statement was added to the card on his desk and became the second question the teacher asked of him each time he had a talking problem. The solution for the teacher needed to be simple because the teacher is very busy in class, but once the plan was established, it went like this.

The teacher came over to the table where Jack was talking and said, "Jack, mark down talking." Jack would then add a tally mark to his talking chart.

"What should you be saying to yourself?"

"Wait quietly."

"Why?"

"Because I want to be known as a guy who is thoughtful about others."

"Okay, let's keep working on it."

Mom and Dad were pleased to hear positive reports in just a few days. Jack was making some significant progress. If, by the way, Jack wouldn't have made changes, then we would have added to the plan with other techniques, practice sessions, and consequences, but he did make changes, so the additions weren't necessary. He just needed an action plan.

Helping children change requires work. A good word that describes that work is therapy. Although the word "therapy" isn't used in our English Bible, the Greek word "Therapeuo" is used regularly to describe the healing work of Christ. (Matthew 4:23, 12:15, 17:18, Mark 1:34, 6:5, Luke 6:18, 9:6, John 5:10) The idea behind the word is "to cure," and the work we do with our kids helps them get well in particular areas of their hearts. It's not one large consequence that usually brings about change. It's the continual heart work that produces lasting results.

Have a Meeting with Your Child

Choose an area for your child to work on. Then approach the problem in a positive way. Larry expressed the problem he had with his four-, eight-, and ten-year-old children this way, "I think my kids use selective listening. I need some advice to get them to listen and obey. In particular, they tend to react to me when they don't want to do what I ask." The kids were each at different developmental stages of life and would require unique approaches. He started with his ten-year-old by using the three C's. Larry said, "Son, I know you're struggling with your response when I give you an instruction that you don't want to do. I discovered a solution that I think might be helpful for you. It's the three C's. Can I share it with you?"

> Helping children change requires work. A good word that describes that work is therapy.

After he explained the idea of the arena, then he talked about the first C, cue. "What is the cue that you're in the arena where I've given you an instruction that you don't want to do?"

The answer in cases like this is usually some kind of internal frustration. Kids have internal reactions before the external ones come out. It might be an internal sigh, a desire to roll the eyes, or just a frustration felt in the neck. It also might be a rush of energy into the body caused by frustration or excitement. Those internal cues might be tough for some kids to recognize at first, so Dad might choose to offer a verbal cue that gives a warning that an instruction is coming. "I could call you over before I give you an instruction, or I could just use your name and require that you look at me. What do you think would be a good cue for you to recognize that you're in the arena?"

After his son made his decision, Dad continued. "The second C is conscience and requires that you have words to say to yourself once you recognize the cue. These are specific words for that situation." Larry listened to ideas from his son and then suggested some other ones. Some words that might be helpful would be things such as, "Get ready," "Be flexible," "Take a deep breath," or "Don't react."

The third C is character. The character quality to work on depends on the child. In this case, it might be self-control, flexibility, or graciousness. Defining the quality that fits the situation in practical terms for each child can provide some direction as well.

> What do you think would be a good cue for you to recognize that you're in the arena?

Larry used the same three C approach with is eight-year-old, but he chose a different plan with his youngest son. He felt like the best approach was to use firmness. He practiced with him in order to develop new patterns of responsiveness. The approaches worked well for all his children, and Larry's thoughtfulness helped contribute to the change. In each case, meeting with his kids independently contributed to their understanding of the new expectations and the plan for progress toward their individual goals.

How did your meeting go? What did you learn? What worked?

_____

_____

_____

_____

_____

_____

_____

_____

_____

Growing Together

When you're through changing, you are through period.
Change is part of life.

A good parenting strategy focuses on where you're going, not where you are now. That one truth often changes a family significantly. We recently had this encouraging comment come to us in the mail a few days after one of our live seminars. A thoughtful parent took time to write, and her testimony touched our hearts.

"This biblical approach to the conscience has completely changed the way I work with my kids. I'm surprised at how much I relied on threats and incentives to get my children to do what I wanted them to do. I didn't even realize there was another way to parent. I'm amazed at how powerful it is to work in a way that addresses the heart. My kids are still kids. They still have problems, but I have a much better plan for dealing with them than before. It's so encouraging for me to see them move forward on their own. I see now how I am helping them build internal motivation."

These kinds of testimonies are a treasure for us. We work with parents every week, and we know that all families are different. Children are unique. Parents have different parenting styles and passions, but when it comes to helping children grow out of some of their most difficult problems, there's nothing that does a better job than addressing the heart and building internal motivation in kids.

> A good parenting strategy focuses on where you're going, not where you are now.

Doing Things Differently

Parents who incorporate the conscience into their parenting approach actually do things differently on a day-to-day basis. We're not just talking about having one conversation with your child about the conscience and then going on as before. New tools take the place of much of the intensity that can drain a family's emotional resources.

Gary is a dad in the trenches, and his hard work is paying off. Gary has two kids, Max, age eleven, and Maddie, age nine. The biggest change he's seen in his relationships with his children is less drama and more dialogue. For example, when Max starts yelling and getting upset, Gary refuses to join into the anger episode. Rather, he simply says, "You need to take a break, settle down, and come back and see me when you're ready to talk in a calm voice."

> Parents who incorporate the conscience into their parenting approach actually do things differently on a day-to-day basis.

His son has been diagnosed with Attention Deficit Hyperactivity Disorder. He's strong-willed and has a hard time following instructions. Max doesn't finish his classwork in a timely manner and doesn't seem motivated to change. Gary is working hard and continues to work the action plan with his son.

Max sometimes tries to bait his father, but Dad knows that his son's heart is overwhelmed at times and that parental anger won't produce good results. As part of his plan, Dad sends Max to take a break and requires that he come back to debrief after he settles down. When Max does return after fifteen minutes, or sometimes even longer, Dad sees a change in his countenance. "I can tell that his conscience is working. Max realizes that his emotions got out of control and comes to a place where he's settled. We're still working on his impulse control, but Max knows what's right, and settling down is part of his solution."

Maddie, on the other hand, struggles with dishonesty. She's tempted to lie to get out of trouble or to take something she wants when the answer is "no." Gary has talked about the conscience with Maddie and helped her recognize that dishonesty is the result of internal weakness and that sometimes she doesn't have the strength to match the pressure of the situation.

It's hard for Maddie to admit it when she's lied. When correcting, Dad sometimes requires that his daughter sit down for a bit until she's ready to say, "I lied." The most productive conversations are the ones about the conscience and the inner battle that Maddie faces. She's struggling between the pressure to get out of trouble—something she wants—and a guilty conscience—something she doesn't want. The dialogue between Dad and Maddie reveals that inner struggle that his daughter feels but doesn't know how to put into words.

Gary has quite a ways to go with his kids, but he's encouraged because he feels like he's connecting with their hearts. They aren't just following rules or avoiding punishment. They're learning important lessons about life and wrestling with things on the inside.

At one point, Gary was sitting on a bench watching his kids play at the park. A man walking by Maddie accidentally dropped a five-dollar bill on the ground. Maddie saw it, and Gary just watched to see what she would do. After a few moments of pondering, she picked up the money and ran after the man to give it to him. Gary was proud of his daughter and affirmed her integrity.

Much of what you do as you parent your kids is just like what Gary is doing. He's using a multifaceted approach to help his children move from point A to point B. He's keeping his eyes on the goal and using correction, instruction, and dialogue to train his children.

Take a moment and write two or three long-term goals you have for your child and then imagine how you might start building toward that goal now.

Goal	Current actions
_____	_____
_____	_____
_____	_____
_____	_____

Kids Need to Understand the Map

As you work in your own family, think about the heart. Instead of instituting the latest punishment, consider how you might move your child on a map from point A to point B. Keep your eyes on the goal. Help your child see that together you're working to develop a character quality. It would be helpful for each of your children to know what character goals you're working on with them. Each child has weaknesses, but too much focus on that weakness just tells kids to stop doing the wrong thing instead of focusing on what's right. As you strategize for heart change, you'll pray for significant opportunities to talk about progress toward point B, the goal.

> Help your child see that together you're working to develop a character quality.

Helping children move from point A to point B creates a family dynamic where parents also grow. One of the greatest motivators of spiritual growth is having kids. It's surprising how much selfishness parents see in themselves as they learn to parent their children. The weaknesses of parents often contribute to challenges in family life. Raising children forces parents to look at their own hearts, develop their own consciences, and rely on the Holy Spirit as never before.

Keep in mind that, when you become a believer, God places you at point A and begins moving you to point B in your life. That's the beauty of a heart-based approach. The work you do with your children now emulates the way God wants to work in their hearts as well. Be sure to share the plan with your child. This is no secret. It's most helpful when kids understand what character quality they need to focus on and some of the specific, practical things you're looking for.

Write down three areas where God is growing you right now in your life.

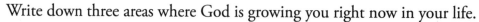

Too many children are raised on simple behavior modification. That approach to life trains kids to think about themselves. When parents help their children practice faith, rely on the Holy Spirit, and pay attention to the promptings of the conscience, they're contributing to the long-term maturity and health of their kids. Parents must often retrain themselves to relate to their kids in more strategic ways, but the work pays off with huge dividends.

Making a Commitment Before God

It's important to realize that the work you do as a parent is about pleasing God, not others. You have a conscience too, and having a clear conscience before God is more important than fitting in or pleasing people. When parents gain that focus, then they have a greater ability to hang in there when things get tough or busy. Parents gain greater determination in the face of resistance. Colossians 3:23-24 is a great passage for any parent to embrace. "Whatever you do, work at it with all your heart, as working for the Lord, not for human masters, since you know that you will receive an inheritance from the Lord as a reward. It is the Lord Christ you are serving."

> The family is a laboratory where God is able to build new character qualities in all family members.

Regularly come to Christ and make him the Lord of your life today. Ask the Holy Spirit to fill you every day. Make your commitment a spiritual one, and your family will benefit from it.[22]

When you become a Christian, God puts you on a course of Christian growth. The family is a laboratory where God is able to build new character qualities in all family members. Are you growing? If so, mark out the milestones and share them with your kids. You might even be bold enough to share with your children where God is taking you next. Take advantage of the opportunities to grow personally and take your child along for the ride. It's an adventure.

Take a few minutes and write out a prayer of commitment before God. First, write down what you believe he is doing in your heart now, and then write down your desire to serve him and grow as he continues to lead in your life.

_____

_____

_____

_____

---

[22] You might want to read Chapter 21 in the book *Motivate Your Child: A Christian Parent's Guide to Raising Kids Who Do What They Need to Do Without Being Told* to get some more fuel for your own spiritual commitment.

_____

_____

_____

_____

_____

Have a Meeting with Your Child

Look for ways to communicate to your child that growth is part of life. One of the greatest ways you can do that is by being vulnerable yourself. What is God teaching you? What is the point B in your life that God is moving you toward? By sharing openly with your child about your own growth, you're helping your child realize that a weakness isn't something to hide or necessarily be ashamed of. Rather, it's a reality in everyone and an opportunity for personal development.

> It's not easy to be vulnerable with kids, especially since you're likely to fail again.

Sometimes parents talk about the growth that they've already accomplished. It's the proverbial, "When I was a child…" conversation. There's nothing wrong with that kind of teaching, but that's not what we're talking about here. Sharing current growth that's not yet complete reveals humility and process instead of having already arrived.

It's not easy to be vulnerable with kids, especially since you're likely to fail again. But let's be honest, your children know you have weaknesses. Kids benefit from knowing that their parents are growing too. Of course, there are areas of your life that may be too personal to share or inappropriate for a child to know about, but, if you look at your life, there's probably something you're learning that would be helpful and encouraging to share with your child.

The goal is to reveal that growth is normal and healthy. It's part of life, and those who resist by arguing, blaming, or justifying themselves don't grow as quickly as those who have courage and humility to admit their weaknesses and move forward.

Look for ways to share honestly with your child. You'll find that the relationship increases, but you'll also see your child become more willing to accept the growth process and be willing to work on change as well.

How did your meeting go? What did you learn? What worked?

_____

_____

_____

_____

_____

_____

_____

Good Theology Makes it Work

We all live with sinful people, even if you live alone. Grace is essential, not optional.

It's important to view children from a biblical perspective and understand how they're designed in order to maximize parenting. The additional thoughts in this chapter provide some theological reflections to ground your parenting.

Christianity vs. Humanism

One of the striking differences between humanism and Christianity has to do with the understanding of the makeup of a person. Humanists tend to believe that people are a higher form of animals. The primary difference between an animal and a human is greater intelligence that they can use to face life challenges. Christianity teaches that God created both people and animals, so you would expect some similarities, but God created each person in the image of God with with a spiritual heart, making humans distinctly different from other created beings. And God has much to say about the heart, what it is and how it functions.

> Anytime a person is motivated to act from the heart, we call that internal motivation.

The human heart is the central processing unit of a person and is the source of internal motivation. Looking at the way the Bible uses the word "heart," we learn that it's the place where many things come together, such as passion, emotion, convictions, values, and desires. It's also the place where people wrestle with things, come to conclusions, and make decisions. The heart develops commitments, and its determination drives a person to act in a particular way. It's also the place where God chooses to live when invited in. He reorients the values, changes desires, and provides direction to what otherwise might be a rather chaotic piece of internal equipment.

Anytime a person is motivated to act from the heart, we call that internal motivation. Unfortunately, wrong desires or unbridled emotions also flow from the heart, prompting some motivations to be evil or unhelpful. So, here's an important note already stated in this book but important to remember: just because something comes from the heart, doesn't make it good or right. A brother might hit his sister because he's internally motivated by his anger. Internal motivation can be wrong. Therefore, it must be guided. That's why, when God created the human heart, he placed a conscience inside. It's part of a guidance system to keep the heart on track.

The Purpose of the Conscience

Remember that the purpose of the conscience is to reveal to every person that God exists and that there is a right and a wrong. When Paul wrote to the Romans, he explained more fully what salvation is. In Romans 2, he addressed the question of whether Gentiles were held accountable to God since they didn't know about him like the Jewish people did.

Paul revealed the answer in Romans 2:14-15, "Indeed, when Gentiles, who do not have the law, do by nature things required by the law, they are a law for themselves, even though they do not have the law. They show that the requirements of the law are written on their hearts, their consciences also bearing witness, and their thoughts sometimes accusing them and at other times even defending them." The conscience is an internal witness that prompts people to see their need for God.

> The conscience is on a mission, and only when it finds salvation through Jesus Christ is it satisfied.

In this book, we've shared practical ways to train the conscience in children in order to build internal motivation. Everyone has a conscience. Even people who don't believe in God or haven't heard the message of salvation have a built-in sensitivity to the fact that there's a God because God placed that knowledge inside the heart by way of the conscience. It's fair to say that God placed the conscience inside a person to provide an internal motivation to find God and give one's heart to him. The conscience is on a mission, and only when it finds salvation through Jesus Christ is it satisfied.

Of course, some people seek to appease the conscience by various means. Some even try religious practices, thinking that, by ceremony or external worship, they will be able to find satisfaction deep in their hearts. The book of Hebrews speaks to this misguided thinking. In Hebrews 9, God helps us understand how important Jesus Christ is and how ultimate satisfaction comes through him, not through religious practices.

The Old Testament provided many religious duties that involved sacrifices, the tabernacle, and priests assisting people in their worship. About this religious system, Hebrews 9:9 says, "This is an illustration for the present time, indicating that the gifts and sacrifices being offered were not able to clear the conscience of the worshiper."

Religiosity doesn't satisfy the built-in need of the human heart. In fact, there's nothing that can appease the conscience like salvation. Some try to do good works, care for the poor, give money, and develop a life of service. Although those things are great, they don't adequately solve the problem of human guilt and a need for a Savior.

Some people blame problems on others or rationalize or justify their offenses in an attempt to defend themselves from a guilty conscience. Those techniques don't work either. People may try to balance the scales of justice by getting personal revenge or by fighting injustice, yet, even when justice is served, the human heart is left lacking. The only solution for a troubled conscience is salvation through Jesus Christ as Lord.

Hebrews 9:14 further describes the solution. "How much more, then, will the blood of Christ, who through the eternal Spirit offered himself unblemished to God, cleanse our consciences from acts that lead to death, so that we may serve the living God!" The conscience is cleansed and, therefore, satisfied when one personally accepts salvation through Jesus Christ. Many people, when they come to a saving knowledge of Christ, describe their experience as a weight lifted

off of their shoulders. That's a description of the cleansing of the conscience through salvation. The heart is now free, released from guilt, and ready to live life with greater joy.

It's important to realize that every person has a sin nature that corrupts the human heart and pollutes the conscience. That's why salvation is so important in a person's life. A humanistic approach suggests that people are basically good, and they just need education to train them and things will be fine. The Bible also encourages training of children, even before they come to know Christ personally, but the greatest contributor to change in a person's life is total commitment to God. Any discussion of the heart or conscience without an understanding of the importance of the gospel would be incomplete and misleading.

When describing salvation, Hebrews 10:22 says, "Let us draw near to God with a sincere heart and with the full assurance that faith brings, having our hearts sprinkled to cleanse us from a guilty conscience and having our bodies washed with pure water." Moral development is incomplete without an emphasis on faith, salvation, God's grace, and his standard, the Bible. The primary function of the conscience is to prompt people to see the need for Christ's work and to motivate them to invite Jesus into their hearts.

The Value of the Conscience After Salvation

After salvation, what use is the conscience? Is that the end of its purpose? Not according to the Bible. In fact, salvation's work to cleanse the conscience is only the beginning. The conscience then becomes a tool for life, and this gives us opportunity to use it with children to strengthen their internal motivation. Paul had been a believer for many years before he made this statement, in Acts 24:16, "So I strive always to keep my conscience clear before God and man."

Paul knew the value of a clear conscience and understood that work was required to keep it that way. In fact, it becomes so important that Paul raised it to the highest level as a tool for faithfulness to God. As he trained Timothy to be a young pastor and to handle himself well, both personally and as a leader in God's church, he described the importance of the conscience, not just once, but three times.

Paul told Timothy to guard against false teaching in the church. He provided the basis for his instruction by saying, "The goal of this command is love, which comes from a pure heart and a good conscience and a sincere faith." (1 Timothy 1:5) A good conscience was something that would help Timothy be a better pastor and to live his life faithfully in the service of God.

In 1 Timothy 1:19, Paul described the danger of abandoning a clear conscience. He said, "Holding on to faith and a good conscience which some have rejected and so have shipwrecked with regards to their faith."

When speaking of the qualifications of a deacon, Paul told Timothy, "They must keep hold of the deep truths of the faith with a clear conscience." (1 Timothy 3:9) Having a clear conscience was, and still is, an important leadership quality.

Paul used the word conscience nineteen times in the New Testament, if you include the instances in the book of Acts that he shared his faith with others. Paul relied on his conscience to help him live life and described how he did that in 2 Timothy 1:3, "I thank God, whom I serve, as my ancestors did, with a clear conscience, as night and day I constantly remember you in my prayers."

The extent of a conscience's usefulness is directly related to a person's willingness to train it and to allow God to equip it. The Bible uses adjectives to describe the conscience, including clear (Acts 24:16, 2 Timothy 1:3), weak (1 Corinthians 8:7), good (1 Timothy 1:5), guilty (Hebrews 10:22), seared (1 Timothy 4:2), and corrupted (Titus 1:15). Those words indicate the importance of holding the conscience with care, responding quickly to its promptings, and allowing God to train it for effectiveness.

> Having a clear conscience was, and still is, an important leadership quality.

The Conscience's Role in the Development of Internal Motivation

God designed the conscience to keep the heart going in the right direction. The heart provides internal motivation; the conscience prompts the heart so that the internal motivation stays on the right path. However, the conscience itself is only a tool. It's not the ultimate standard for right and wrong. Paul made that clear in 1 Corinthians 4:4 when he said, "My conscience is clear, but that does not make me innocent. It is the Lord who judges me."

A child who just got revenge might feel a temporary sense of satisfaction and an appeased conscience. That doesn't justify the actions. A person might feel at peace about disobedience to God. That doesn't make it right.

The conscience needs training. For that reason, God leaves another space in the human heart to complete the internal guidance system. The conscience is maximized by the presence of God himself living and residing inside us. 1 Corinthians 3:16 asks the rhetorical question, "Don't you know that you yourselves are God's temple and that God's Spirit dwells in your midst?" When a person accepts Jesus as Lord and Savior, then the Holy Spirit takes up residence inside the heart.

Some people mistakenly believe that the Holy Spirit and the conscience are the same thing. They aren't, and many of the verses in this chapter alone indicate the unique identity of each. The conscience is a human element inside every person. It's standard operating equipment for everyone, young and old. The Holy Spirit is a person who comes to live in the heart at the second birth, which the Bible calls salvation. The Holy Spirit doesn't take the place of the conscience, but rather, further equips it to do the work it needs to do.

Internal Motivation is Powerful

Steve and Trudi realized that the first thing they needed to do to make some changes was to teach their twelve-year-old son, Curt, about the conscience and the Holy Spirit. They had some parenting work to do and needed a strategy for building responsibility. They agreed starting with internal motivation for a couple of weeks seemed like a better approach than jumping into correction.

Curt wasn't motivated. His parents had to tell him what to do every step of the way. They were frustrated, saying to themselves, "He's twelve. He ought to be able to manage himself better than this." Steve and Trudi set out to develop an action plan that took Curt's unique personality and needs into account. They didn't want to start out negatively, because they felt like they had been nagging him for years already.

They were on the lookout to see something that their son did without prompting, some example of responsibility. The next day, they got their chance. Curt saw that one of the trashcans outside had blown over. He picked up the trash, put it in the can, and moved the can to a more secure place. They were impressed, but more importantly, this was exactly the kind of self-prompted action they were waiting for.

Dad said to Curt, "Son, I saw that you fixed that trash problem outside. Thank you. I'm impressed and grateful. I want to ask you a question. Since you did that without someone telling you to, I was wondering what prompted you to fix it. Was it your conscience, or was it the Holy Spirit?"

Curt looked at Dad as if he was crazy, but the comment provided the opportunity for Dad to do some teaching about internal motivation and explain some things about the heart. Of course, many times it's hard to tell whether the internal prompting came from the conscience, the Holy Spirit, or just some other desire of the heart. The point is that Curt was internally motivated. The more sensitive he is to those internal urges, the more effective he'll be in relationships, at work, at school, and in his personal life.

During the dialogue, Curt's initial response indicated that he thought the conscience only had to do with avoiding bad things. He had this image that the conscience was just there to thump him on the side of the head. When his parents

shared that the conscience provides internal promptings in several areas, including being responsible, Curt thought it was interesting. Dad explained to Curt the three levels of thinking. The first level is just thinking about what you're doing now, your current activity. It might be eating, playing a video game, or talking to your friend. Level 2 thinking asks responsibility questions. This was important for Curt as he was learning to ask, "What else should I be doing? Did I leave a mess somewhere? How can I help out around here?"

The idea of Level 3 thinking was intriguing for Curt. That's the level that asks, "What is God doing right now?" Sometimes it was seeing what God was doing in his own life, and other times it was considering what God was doing elsewhere, but it became an important point of dialogue between him and his parents.

Dad, Mom, and Curt needed to think of new ways to approach tasks in life. They still had more questions, but they were headed in the right direction.

Learning more about the Holy Spirit's daily work would be a key component for them.

The Holy Spirit has a powerful influence on internal motivation. The scriptures reveal that the work of God in a person's life does many things that empower the conscience. God convicts of sin (John 16:8), provides forgiveness (1 John 1:9), helps fight temptation (1 Corinthians 10:13), provides power to do right and avoid wrong (Ephesians 6:10-18), guides into truth (John 16:13), confirms honesty (Romans 9:1), reminds of the right thing (John 14:26), lives inside believers (John 14:17), and makes God's teaching clear (1 Corinthians 2:10-14). In short, the Holy Spirit works alongside the conscience and affects it in ways that provide a superb guidance system for the heart of a person.

The Holy Spirit has a powerful influence on internal motivation.

Stop for a moment and realize that the study of moral development in children doesn't come from a psychology textbook. It comes from the Bible. Understanding the makeup of a person is useful if you're doing work to help people change. Parents try to help their children mature and develop. You aren't alone in your work to train your child. If you can work alongside God's existing work, you can have a greater impact on your child's development.

Maybe you're saying to yourself, "This all makes sense for an adult. I get it. The conscience prompts a person to salvation, and that in turn cleanses the conscience. Then, God guides a person through a growing conscience and the work of the Holy Spirit to live for him. But what about kids? First of all, many children aren't Christians yet. How does all of this work with children who are going through developmental stages?"

That's a good question. The Bible teaches that we treat young children as part of God's family and train them to follow the Lord, while at all times appealing to them to make a personal commitment to Jesus. That's why, for example, you take your children to church each week. If your kids say, "I don't want to go to church," you don't say, "Okay, because your heart isn't in it, you don't have to go." Rather, you take them whether they like it or not. Children are learning what it means to follow God, before they fully understand the implications. You'll likely teach your preschooler to pray even before she makes a public commitment to Christ.

In the same way, you'll train your child's conscience long before she fully understands the work of the Holy Spirit. When you teach your daughter to take out the trash and put a new liner in the can, and she becomes able to do it on her own without being reminded, then you've successfully created inside her a right and a wrong way of dealing with the trash. The daily training parents do contributes to a powerful line inside the human heart between right and wrong. Sometimes those are moral lines, but other times they are simply the proper way to do something. Kids learn to say "thank you" when they receive a gift, how to be excused from the table, or to turn off the light when finished in the bathroom. Those actions require training and involve the conscience as a prompter to do them.

Your early influence and training will set the stage for spiritual awakening and growth. Some parents say, "I'll wait until my children are older to let them choose what faith they want to follow." The only parents who say that are ones who don't know the truth or recognize that there is only one God, and that living for him is the only way to truly be satisfied. The greatest job of any parent is to help kids be disciples of Jesus Christ. It starts with early training to prepare the way for personal commitment to God.

Furthermore, the Holy Spirit works in people even before they commit themselves to Christ. Jesus tells his disciples in John 16:7-8, "Unless I go away, the Advocate will not come to you; but if I go, I will send him to you. When he comes, he will prove the world to be in the wrong about sin and righteousness and judgment." Notice that the Holy Spirit is working on nonbelievers. The primary call is to come to salvation, but the Holy Spirit's convicting work takes place in small, practical ways each day toward that greater end. Even before a person commits himself to Jesus Christ, the Holy Spirit is working, prompting, and initiating inside. Parents can help their children understand and recognize the voice of the Holy Spirit in their hearts even at an early age.

> The greatest job of any parent is to help kids be disciples of Jesus Christ.

Curt had never considered the fact that God cared about his homework or that the Holy Spirit would help him complete a task without reminders. This was new territory for him, and it was helping Curt think more broadly about his own heart and the practicality of his faith. Dad and Mom were getting somewhere, and they started to see Curt take initiative in other areas, doing things without being told. It was simple things, like cleaning up after himself, that demonstrated the work of the conscience inside. Curt has a long way to go, but hearing this teaching opened new ways for him to think about life.

Steve and Trudi are learning a new way to parent that's heart-directed, and it often requires some adjustment in their thinking and behavior. It's amazing how many of us have been greatly influenced by secular humanism. Some parents go so far as to train their children as if they're animals by inadvertently overemphasizing rewards and punishment.

When that happens, parents miss the tremendous opportunities that a heart-based approach to parenting offers. Parents who understand their faith, realize that there's another large bucket of parenting tools that is heart-related. They help their children make progress more quickly and see them making lasting changes, as well.

You may want to reread this chapter and look up all the verses. In fact, there are a number of Bible studies found just in this chapter that provide good meditation material for parents.

Always remember, it's important to start with good theology if you want to end up with good techniques.

May God richly bless you as you work to build internal motivation in the heart of your child. We continue to enjoy the testimonies that parents share with us. Maybe you'd consider taking time to write to us and tell us what God is doing in you and your home.

Blessings,

Dr. Scott Turansky and Joanne Miller, RN, BSN

parent@biblicalparenting.org

P.S. If you'd like to have fun with your kids and teach them about the Bible in exciting ways, you might want to look at the Family Time Activities Books at biblicalparenting.org. Kids beg for more when you teach the Bible with activity. For example, to illustrate the story in Daniel 3 about Shadrach, Meshach, and Abednego, who were thrown into the fiery furnace, you might want do an activity where you light three cardboard men on fire. Once they've

Kids beg for more when you teach the Bible with activity.

been soaked in the alcohol/water solution according to the recipe in the **Seeing is Believing** book in that series, then you'll have some real excitement on your hands.

Have fun with God's Word. It's a great gift to give to your kids.

Everyday Parents **CAN** Raise Extraordinary Kids!

Video Series

by Dr. Scott Turansky and Joanne Miller, RN, BSN

Parents learn to help their children be internally motivated instead of relying on parental prompters in four areas: Doing what's right, Dealing with wrongs, Being honest, and Caring about others. Join Dr. Turansky and Mrs. Miller as they teach parents about the biblical concept of the conscience and encourage its development.

When you

focus

on the
conscience,
good things
happen!

8 Packed Sessions • 21 Parenting Strategies
Rooted in Theology • Amazingly Practical
You'll see change in 30 days whether your child
is 3 or 18

- Learn how a heart-based approach differs from behavior modification
- Understand the difference between the conscience and the Holy Spirit—and how to take advantage of both in parenting
- Identify your own convictions and learn how to teach them to your kids
- Teach children to take initiative and be responsible
- Apply these principles to parenting children of any age
- Understand Attention Deficit Disorder and provide kids with hope
- Using five tools, develop a plan for change in 30 days
- Coach children to handle their emotions
- Help kids respond better to correction
- Develop honesty in practical ways

Parenting is **Heart WORK**

NATIONAL CENTER for BIBLICAL Parenting

76 Hopatcong Drive, Lawrenceville, NJ 08648-4136
Phone: (609) 771-8002
Order online at: biblicalparenting.org

HERO TRAINING CAMP

The Conscience Development Program for Kids ages 3-12

Hero Training Camp uses the life of David, activities, songs, crafts, and science experiments to teach children what it means to be a hero now in four areas: do what's right, deal with wrongs, be honest, and care about others.

For Children Ages 3-12

Teaching Children How to Be Heroes in Everyday Life

HERO TRAINING CAMP

HERO IN TRAINING

An activity-based biblical study of the conscience for kids. Use in the home, in groups, or as VBS or Family VBS.

By Dr. Scott Turansky and Joanne Miller, RN, BSN

Kids will learn how to handle mistakes and offenses, face the challenge of being honest under pressure, take initiative to help others, how to be a one minute hero, and the skill of seeing things that need to be done and doing them. These are all qualities of heroes. The training starts now!

NATIONAL CENTER for BIBLICAL Parenting

76 Hopatcong Drive, Lawrenceville, NJ 08648-4136
Phone: (609) 771-8002
Order online at: biblicalparenting.org